DATE DUE

DOS INSTANT
REFERENCE

The SYBEX Prompter Series

We've designed the SYBEX Prompter Series to meet the evolving needs of software users, who want essential information presented in an accessible format. Our best authors have distilled their expertise into compact *Instant Reference* books you can use to look up the precise use of any command—its syntax, available options, and operation. More than just summaries, these books also provide realistic examples and insights into effective usage drawn from our authors' wealth of experience.

The SYBEX Prompter Series also includes these titles:

Lotus 1-2-3 Instant Reference
Greg Harvey and Kay Yarborough Nelson

WordPerfect Instant Reference
Greg Harvey and Kay Yarborough Nelson

dBASE Instant Reference
Alan Simpson

Turbo BASIC Instant Reference
Douglas Hergert

The SYBEX Prompter™ Series

DOS® INSTANT REFERENCE

Greg Harvey
and
Kay Yarborough Nelson

San Francisco • Paris • Düsseldorf • London

SYBEX Prompter Series
Editor in Chief: Rudolph S. Langer
Managing Editor: Barbara Gordon
Series Editor: James A. Compton
Editor: Tanya Kucak

Cover design by Thomas Ingalls + Associates

AT&T is a trademark of AT&T Corporation.
Burroughs is a trademark of Burroughs Corporation.
Compaq is a trademark of Compaq Computer Corporation.
dBASE III PLUS is a trademark of Ashton-Tate, Inc.
IBM, Proprinter, Enhanced Graphics Adapter (EGA), Convertible LCD, PC-DOS, Personal Computer AT, PC XT, PS/2, Portable PC, Quietwriter III, and TopView are trademarks of International Business Machines Corporation.
Intel is a trademark of Intel Corporation.
Lightning, SideKick, and SuperKey are trademarks of Borland International.
Lotus 1-2-3 is a trademark of Lotus Development Corporation.
MS-DOS is a trademark of Microsoft Corporation.
Mace Utilities is a trademark of Paul Mace Software.
Norton Utilities is a trademark of Peter Norton Computing.
WordPerfect is a trademark of WordPerfect Corporation.
WordStar and WordStar 2000 are trademarks of MicroPro Corporation.

SYBEX is a registered trademark and Prompter Series is a trademark of SYBEX, Inc.

SYBEX is not affiliated with any manufacturer.

Every effort has been made to supply complete and accurate information. However, SYBEX assumes no responsibility for its use, nor for any infringements of patents or other rights of third parties which would result.

Library of Congress Card Number: 87-63039
ISBN 0-89588-477-1
Manufactured in the United States of America
10 9 8 7 6 5

ACKNOWLEDGMENTS

Many thanks to Judd Robbins, author of *Mastering DOS* (SYBEX, 1988), for the information in Appendices C, D, and E.

Thanks are due to the following people at SYBEX: Dr. Rudolph Langer and Alan Oakes for furnishing the inspiration for this project; Dr. Rodnay Zaks, president, for valuable advice; Jim Compton, the Prompter Series editor; Barbara Gordon, managing editor; Tanya Kucak, copy editor; John Kadyk and Maria Mart, word processing; Ingrid Owen, design; Liberty Batol, design and pasteup; Cheryl Vega, typesetting; and Aidan Wylde, proofreading.

TABLE OF CONTENTS

Introduction

The idea behind this book is simple: when you are stymied by a DOS command that does not work as you intended or one that produces unpredicted results, or if you want a quick refresher about a certain procedure, you need a single source of information that can help you quickly solve the problem at hand so that you can get on with your work.

This *DOS Instant Reference* is intended to serve just that purpose: to give you in as short a space as possible the essential information necessary to use the DOS commands—both the basic commands as well as those more sophisticated commands that you probably do not use every day. It covers both PC-DOS (up to and including version 3.3) and MS-DOS (up to and including version 3.2) of the program; commands found only in PC-DOS version 3.30 are marked with a *3.3* symbol.

The *DOS Instant Reference* provides you with an alphabetical listing of all of the DOS commands from APPEND to XCOPY. Each command reference entry starts with a short description of the function of the command, followed by a listing of the versions of DOS (both PC-DOS and MS-DOS) that it runs under. Next comes the TYPE, which indicates whether the command is internal (kept in RAM) or external (kept on the DOS disk until executed).

Following the version and type information, you will see the SYNTAX (format) of the DOS command. The syntax section utilizes essentially the same conventions used in your DOS documentation, with slight variations. (For example, where the DOS documentation uses *d:* in a syntax line to signify the source drive, and then again to signify the target, we've distinguished different drives by using *sd:* and *td:*, respectively.) According to these conventions, optional parameters are always enclosed in square brackets. For example, in

DIR   [*d:*][*path*][*filename*][/**P**][/**W**]

the *d:*, *path*, *filename*, /P, and /W parameters are not required to get a directory listing of the files on the (default) drive and are, therefore, enclosed in square brackets.

Also, all variable information in the command is shown in italics in the syntax command line. In the DIR command example, the optional *d:*, *path*, and *filename* parameters are shown in italics to indicate that you substitute the letter of the drive, the name of the path, and indicate the file name(s) when you want a directory listing either from a drive or directory that differs from that of the default or you want just a directory of a particular file or group of files.

For example, if you want a directory listing of the files on a disk in drive A, and drive C is the default drive, you enter

DIR A:

where A: stands for the [*d:*] variable in the syntax command line.

Many DOS commands offer you numerous optional parameters (this is especially true for version 3.30). To help you decipher what at first may appear as a tremendously complex command syntax, an OPTIONS section follows the syntax entry. It is here that you will find all of the command's options explained at a glance.

The OPTIONS section is followed by EXAMPLES that illustrate typical command usage and the most common DOS prompt and error messages that you may see when using the command. Note that the prompt and error messages shown in the MESSAGES section are arranged in alphabetical order.

Depending upon the particular DOS command, the EXAMPLES and MESSAGES may be followed by an UNDO section that explains how to recover from an error or reset the system to the default setting, a NOTES section that alerts you to any peculiarities of the command, and, finally, a SEE ALSO section that cross-references the command being discussed with other DOS commands, or directs you to one of the appendices.

Following the DOS command reference entries, you will find two appendices. Appendix A discusses the creation and use of batch files. This discussion includes the special AUTOEXEC.BAT file as well as all of the special batch file commands provided by DOS.

Appendix B discusses the creation and use of the CONFIG.SYS file, which allows you to configure the DOS environment to better suit your computer system. This discussion covers all of the parameters that are under your control when setting up the CONFIG.SYS file, as well as the special configuration commands used to set up new values.

APPEND
Locating Application Files

Searches a specified path to locate files outside of the current directory that have extensions other than .COM, .EXE, or .BAT.

VERSION

PC-DOS 3.3

TYPE

External/Internal

SYNTAX

To load:

   [*d:***][***path***] APPEND** *sd:spath* **[;[***sd:***]***spath* . . .**]**

or

   [*d:***][***path***] APPEND [/X][/E]**

After loading:

   APPEND *sd:spath* **[;[***sd:***]***spath* . . .**]**

or

   APPEND[;]

OPTIONS	
d:path	Specifies the drive letter and path that contain the APPEND command.
sd:spath	Specifies the drive letter and path to search. Paths cannot be specified the first time the APPEND command is invoked if either the /X or /E parameter is used.
;	Separates APPEND paths; without another parameter, cancels the APPEND list.
/X	Processes functions that require file searches (such as COMP) or DOS commands.
/E	Searches the DOS environment each time the command is issued. Specifically, /E causes the APPEND path to be stored in the environment, and searched for there.

APPEND allows you to store application programs on a hard disk so that you can run them without changing to the directory that contains them. APPEND is useful with programs that need to find overlays, such as help files. Otherwise, the PATH command suffices.

EXAMPLES	

APPEND   /E/X

loads APPEND, specifying that the environment be searched for the APPEND string each time APPEND is used (for example, to see if it has been changed with the SET command) and that file-searching and executive functions operate. After APPEND is loaded, the command

APPEND   C:\PROGS

specifies that all programs stored in the directory named PROGS can be used as if they were in the current directory.

APPEND already installed

The APPEND command is already internal. Issue the command without a path name preceding it so that the internal version will be used.

APPEND / ASSIGN conflict

The APPEND command must be loaded before you load ASSIGN.

APPEND / TopView conflict

TopView must be loaded after APPEND. Exit from TopView and reload APPEND before attempting to reenter TopView.

Incorrect APPEND version

You are using a version of APPEND that does not match the version you first loaded. Check your PATH setting and change the path to locate the correct APPEND version.

Invalid path or file name

You specified a name that does not exist. Check the name and try again.

Invalid path or parameter

You specified a path name as well as the /X and/or /E options. The /X and /E options can only be specified the first time you use APPEND and cannot be used with a path name.

NO APPEND

APPEND is not currently in effect; it was previously issued with ; as the append path.

UNDO

Issue the command

APPEND ;

to cancel the APPEND list.

NOTES

APPEND must be loaded before you load any application programs that you wish to use without changing directories. Once APPEND has been loaded, it becomes an internal command, and you do not have to enter a path before the APPEND command. The /X and /E options can be used only the first time you use APPEND. If you are not specifying the /X or /E options, you may specify the APPEND search path at the same time that you load APPEND. Do not use the /E option if you have loaded a second command processor. Also, /X is not recommended for use with BACKUP and can give misleading results with DIR and TREE. If you have loaded APPEND with the /X option, you must reset the APPEND path by using the ; option before using BACKUP and RESTORE. You can append as many directories as can be specified within 128 characters. The directory you specify in the search path is searched first, followed by the rest of the specified directories. If you do not specify a directory, the current directory is searched. Appended directories may be local or remote.

SEE ALSO

BACKUP
PATH
RESTORE

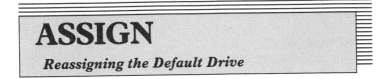

ASSIGN
Reassigning the Default Drive

Instructs DOS to use a disk drive other than the one originally specified by an application program.

VERSION

PC-DOS 2.0 +
MS-DOS equivalent: **ASSIGN** (3.0 +)

TYPE

External

SYNTAX

[*d:*][*path*] **ASSIGN** *d1* = *d2*

OPTIONS

d:path	Before ASSIGN, specifies the drive letter and path that contain the ASSIGN command.
d1	Specifies the current drive letter to which disk I/O requests are sent.
d2	Specifies the drive letter to which disk I/O requests are now to be sent.

ASSIGN allows you to reassign the default drive before running a program that includes drive names in the files it accesses so that you can run drive-specific version 1 programs on a hard disk.

ASSIGN A = B

assigns drive A to drive B so that whenever drive A is requested, drive B is used.

ASSIGN A = C B = C

assigns both drive A and drive B to drive C.

ASSIGN

reassigns the default settings so that requests for drive C go to that drive.

| UNDO |

Issue the ASSIGN command.as

ASSIGN

with no parameters to return drives to their normal assignments.

| NOTES |

Be careful to reassign drives to their normal assignments before running another program that contains drive designations. If you reassign the designation of the drive that contains the ASSIGN program, you cannot clear the assignment without rebooting. Do not use ASSIGN with the BACKUP, RESTORE, LABEL, JOIN, SUBST, or PRINT command. In addition, FORMAT, DISK-COPY, and DISKCOMP ignore drive reassignments.

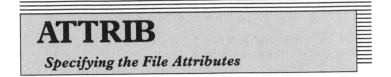

ATTRIB

Specifying the File Attributes

Allows you to specify a file as read-only or archived, or to display whether a file has either of these attributes.

VERSION

PC-DOS 3.0 + (revised in 3.3)
MS-DOS equivalent: **ATTRIB** (3.0 +)

TYPE

External

SYNTAX

[*d:*][*path*] **ATTRIB** [+ R][– R][+ A][– A]
 [*cd:*][*cpath*]*cfilename* **/S**

OPTIONS

d:path	Specifies the drive letter and path that contain the ATTRIB command.
+R	Sets file to read-only.
−R	Removes read-only status.
+A	Sets the archive bit for the file.
−A	Turns off the archive bit for the file.
cd:cpath *cfilename*	Specifies the file whose attribute you are changing.

/S   Instructs DOS to set attributes for all files in the subdirectories of the directory.

ATTRIB is used in networks in which multiple users need to be able to access certain files but not alter them.

EXAMPLES

ATTRIB +R DATA.TXT

BEFORE: Allows read or write access.
AFTER: Sets the file DATA.TXT to read-only.

To view the status of that file (to see whether it has been marked read-only), enter

ATTRIB DATA.TXT

DOS returns the line

R A:\DATA.TXT

indicating by the R that the file has been marked read-only.

MESSAGE

Invalid path or file name

You specified a name that does not exist. Check the path name and try again.

UNDO

To remove the restricted access, enter the command as in

ATTRIB −R DATA.TXT

Use the command

ATTRIB −A C:*.* /S

to reset (turn off) the archive bit for all files in all subdirectories on drive C.

NOTES

The file name may contain a path and extension, and wildcards may be used. If you want to use the files with the BACKUP, RESTORE, and XCOPY commands with the /M option, or the XCOPY command with the /A option, use the +A option if necessary to set the archive bit. If the archive bit is not set, files will not be copied when these commands are used. In PC-DOS version 3.3, you can modify attributes for selected files in a directory or subdirectory.

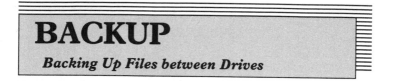

BACKUP
Backing Up Files between Drives

Backs up files from one disk to another disk in another drive, usually from a hard disk to a floppy disk.

VERSION

PC-DOS 2.0 + (revised in 3.3)
MS-DOS equivalent: **BACKUP** (2.0 +)

TYPE

External

SYNTAX

[*d:*][*path*] **BACKUP** *sd:*[*spath*]*sfilename* *td:*[/**S**][/**M**][/**A**]
[/**D**:*mm-dd-yy*][/**T**:*hh:mm:ss*][/**F**][/**L**[:[*ld:*][*l/path*]*lfilename*]]

OPTIONS

d:path	Specifies the drive letter and path that contain the BACKUP command.
sd:	Specifies the drive letter of the drive that contains the file you wish to back up (source).
spath sfilename	Specifies the names of the file or files you wish to back up (source).
td:	Specifies the drive letter of the drive that will contain the files that you wish to back up (target).

/S	Backs up all files in all subdirectories.
/M	Backs up only those files that have been created or altered since the last backup.
/A	Adds files to the disk in the designated drive without overwriting any files that may already be on the disk.
/D:*mm-dd-yy*	Backs up only those files that have been altered on or after the date specified.
/T:*hh:mm:ss*	Backs up files that have been altered on or after the specified time on the date used in option D.
/F	Formats the target disk if it has not been formatted.
/L	Creates a log file in which the first record contains the backup date and time, and subsequent records contain the disk number of each backed-up file as well as its full path name.
ld:lpath lfilename	Specifies the log file. The default log file is BACKUP.LOG, which is stored in the root directory (DOS 3.3 only).

EXAMPLES

BACKUP C:*.* A:/S

backs up all the files on drive C, including those in subdirectories, to the disk in drive A.

BACKUP C:*.* A:/S/M

backs up only those files that have been modified since the last backup.

BACKUP C:*pathname* A:/A

appends the backed-up files from the specified directory to the files that are on the disk in drive A without overwriting them.

BACKUP   C:*.*   A:/S/D:12-15-87

backs up all the files on drive C that were created or modified later than 12-15-87 to a disk in drive A.

BACKUP   C: A:/F

formats the disk in drive A before backing up files.

BACKUP   C:\   B:/S/L

backs up all files on drive C to a disk in drive B while creating a BACKUP.LOG file in the drive C root directory.

| MESSAGES |

* * * Backing up files to diskette *xx* * * *

The backup procedure is in progress.

Cannot execute FORMAT

DOS cannot find FORMAT in the current directory or path, or there is insufficient memory to load FORMAT. Press Ctrl-C to abort the backup. Then insert a formatted disk and reissue the BACKUP command.

Cannot FORMAT nonremovable drive *x*

You specified the /F option but the target disk is a hard disk or network drive.

Diskette is not a backup diskette

The diskette that is being used for backup with the /A option was not created by using the BACKUP command. Issue the BACKUP command without the /A option, which overwrites the floppy disk, or insert the correct disk in the drive and reissue the BACKUP command with the /A option again.

Error opening log file

You specified the /L option, but an error such as an invalid drive or path or a file-sharing conflict occurred. Check to see that the drive and path you specified for the log file are valid. The log file must not be on the target disk.

Insert backup diskette *nn* in drive *x;*
Warning! Diskette files will be erased
Strike any key when ready

Insert the next backup disk in the correct drive; then press any key to continue backing up files.

Insert last backup diskette in drive *x*

You are using the /A option. Insert the last backup target disk you used.

Invalid drive specification
Source and Target drives are the same

You cannot specify the same drive as both the source and the target.

* * * Last file not backed up * * *

The target disk was filled and there was no room for the last file.

Logging to file *x*

DOS is creating a log file as you specified.

No source drive specified

You did not specify a source drive. Issue the command again with both source and target drives.

* * * Not able to back up file * * *

A file-sharing conflict exists, and files cannot be backed up. Reissue the request with the /M option. You may have attempted to back up a file to which you do not have access.

Target cannot be used for BACKUP

If the target is a floppy disk, remove it and insert another. If it is not a floppy disk, restart the system and try again.

Warning! No files were found to back up

DOS could not find any files that matched the specifications of the BACKUP command that was issued.

Warning! Files in the target drive
d:BACKUP directory will be erased
Strike any key when ready

Press Ctrl-Break if you do not want to proceed; otherwise, press any key to proceed.

UNDO

Use the RESTORE command to copy backed-up files onto the hard disk.

NOTES

Backed-up files cannot be used as normal files. If files used in a backup fill one disk, you will be prompted to insert another. You will need to have a supply of formatted disks on hand. Be sure to label the disks in proper sequence so that they can be restored in order. To restore backed-up files to the hard disk, use the RESTORE command. Wildcards may be used with the BACKUP command. Do not use BACKUP with the ASSIGN, APPEND, or JOIN command. You may also back up files by using the DISKCOPY or COPY command.

PC-DOS 3.3 contains a revised BACKUP command that stores files more efficiently than previous versions by creating special files that contain information about the backed-up files and their locations, and by concatenating them into a single backup file per disk. In version 3.3 of PC-DOS, you can also back up files that have been altered on or after a specific time, and format the target disk while backing up.

SEE ALSO

COPY
DISKCOPY
RESTORE
XCOPY

BREAK

Checking Whether Break Was Invoked

Controls circumstances under which DOS checks for the Ctrl-C or Break key (Ctrl-Break on the IBM PC) while programs are executing.

VERSION

PC-DOS 2.0 +
MS-DOS equivalent: **BREAK** (2.0 +)

TYPE

Internal

SYNTAX

BREAK [ON | OFF]

OPTIONS

ON   Sets BREAK to on. BREAK ON allows interruption of programs while they are not performing input or output to the console, the printer, or auxiliary devices.

OFF   Sets BREAK to off (the default).

EXAMPLES

C>BREAK ON

sets BREAK to ON. To see the status of the command, issue it with no argument:

A>BREAK
BREAK is on

NOTES ══════════════════

With BREAK set to OFF, DOS checks only when it performs a
screen or keyboard system call or carries out a printer or other auxiliary device operation. Specifying ON instructs DOS to check to see
whether the Break key combination has been pressed before it performs any system call. You can specify BREAK = ON in your configuration file.

SEE ALSO ═════════════════

Appendix B: The CONFIG.SYS File

CHCP
Changing the Code Page

At the system level, selects the code page DOS is using, which contains character set definitions.

VERSION

PC-DOS 3.3

TYPE

Internal

SYNTAX

CHCP [*xxx*]

OPTIONS

xxx   Specifies the number of the desired code page.

In PC-DOS version 3.3, CHCP is used to switch from the standard code page of 437 to the new code pages containing international symbols provided with this version of DOS.

EXAMPLES

CHCP 850

instructs DOS to use code page 850, which contains the character set definition for multilingual characters.

CHCP
displays the operating-system code page that is currently in effect.

Active codepage: *xxx*
reports the code page DOS is currently using.

Codepages *xxx* not prepared for system
CHCP could not select the page you specified. Make sure that NLS-FUNC is loaded and prepare all devices for the code page by using the MODE command.

PC-DOS 3.3 allows you to switch between different code pages, which contain the definitions of characters that are displayed on the screen or produced by your printer. If you use Canadian French, Norwegian, Danish, or Portuguese, you may want to use code page switching to produce newly supported special characters. The NLSFUNC command must be loaded before you use the CHCP command.

NLSFUNC
MODE

CHDIR (CD)
Changing the Current Directory

Makes a new directory or subdirectory current.

VERSION

PC-DOS 2.0+
MS-DOS equivalent: **CHDIR (CD)** (2.0+)

TYPE

Internal

SYNTAX

CHDIR   [*d:*][*path*]

OPTIONS

d:	Specifies the drive letter of the disk you wish to make current.
path	Specifies the desired directory path name to make current. The path name can be no more than 63 characters, beginning with the root directory designation (\).

EXAMPLES

A>CHDIR   C:\WP\LETTERS

changes to the subdirectory LETTERS on drive C. If no drive is specified, the current drive is assumed.

C>CD

allows you to change to the root directory.

CD ..

makes the current directory the preceding level in the tree.

| UNDO |

To check your current directory, issue the CD command with no arguments. The path name of your current directory will be returned, as in the following example:

C>CD
C:\WP\LETTERS

Then, issue the appropriate CD command to make a new directory current.

| NOTES |

The CHDIR command is usually abbreviated to CD.

| SEE ALSO |

MDIR (MD)
RMDIR (RD)

CHKDSK
Checking the Disk

Reports disk size, space available, and RAM available. Also reports and optionally corrects internal disk errors.

VERSION

PC-DOS 2.0+ (revised from 1.0)
MS-DOS equivalent: **CHKDSK** (2.0+, revised from 1.0)

TYPE

External

SYNTAX

[*d:*][*path*] **CHKDSK** [*cd:*][*cpath*][*cfilename*][/F][/V]

OPTIONS

d:path	Specifies the drive letter and path name containing the CHKDSK command file.
cd:cpath *cfilename*	Specifies the file or files (if wildcards are used) to be checked. If omitted, all files in the current directory are checked.
/F	Fixes errors in the File Allocation Table (FAT).
/V	Provides file names as it examines them so that you can see where errors occur.

CHKDSK is often used to verify the internal organization of a disk or to check the amount of space available. It can also be used to test for fragmented files. With the /F option, CHKDSK can be used to repair common internal disk errors.

CHKDSK

checks drive C, reporting any internal errors as well as disk size, free space, and available RAM.

CHKDSK B:/F

checks the disk in drive B while fixing any internal errors it finds. You will be asked whether you wish to recover any lost data sectors (allocation units) into data files. If you respond Y, each lost allocation unit is recovered into its own file, named FILE*nnn*.CHK. You can inspect the recovered units by using the TYPE or DEBUG command. If they are needed, you can RENAME them again or concatenate them using COPY; if not, you can delete them.

CHKDSK B:REPORTS

checks the file named REPORTS, reporting any noncontiguous areas on the disk that are occupied by the REPORTS file. The more noncontiguous areas CHKDSK reports, the greater the fragmentation on the disk, which reduces disk operation speed. To eliminate fragmentation, issue the BACKUP, FORMAT, and RESTORE commands to back up the disk, reformat it, and then restore the backed-up files to the disk, respectively.

CHKDSK B:/F/V

checks the disk in drive B, repairing it while displaying a series of messages indicating its progress and status.

MESSAGES

All specified file(s) are contiguous

The files you specified are not fragmented (that is, they are not stored in noncontiguous areas).

Cannot CHKDSK a network drive

You cannot use CHKDSK to check a network drive or a disk that is being shared on a network. If the disk is shared, have the server pause and then perform CHKDSK.

Cannot CHKDSK a SUBSTed or ASSIGNed drive

The SUBST command hides information that CHKDSK needs. Remove the substitution and try again.

CHDIR..failed, trying alternate method

CHKDSK could not change directories. Restart DOS and issue the CHKDSK command again.

Convert lost chains to files (Y/N)?

Respond Y to convert lost data blocks to files. If you have used the /F option, each chain will be recovered into a separate file. If you enter N, CHKDSK frees the blocks so that they can be allocated to new files.

Directory is joined,
tree past this point not processed.

The JOIN command has been used to join the drive to another device. CHKDSK skips over joined devices.

Directory to file (Y/N)?

The directory that is being checked contains too much invalid information to continue to be used as a directory. Enter Y to convert the directory to a file that can be examined with DEBUG. Enter N if you do not want the directory to be changed to a file.

Disk error reading/writing FAT *x*

The *x* portion of the FAT could not be updated. If this message appears twice for FATs 1 and 2, format the disk. If FORMAT fails, the disk is probably unusable.

[.].Entry has a bad attribute
(or size or link)

One period preceding this message indicates that the current directory is in error; two periods indicates the parent directory. Use the /F option to correct the error.

Error found, F parameter not specified
Corrections will not be written to disk

CHKDSK is analyzing but not correcting the disk. To correct the disk, use the /F option.

File is cross-linked
on cluster *xx*

The same data block is linked to two different files.

filename Allocation error for file, size adjusted

The file allocation table contains an invalid file allocation unit. The file is truncated after the last valid file allocation unit.

filename Contains invalid cluster
[file truncated]

The file has an invalid pointer. If you have used the /F option, the bracketed message is also reported.

filename Contains *xxx* non-contiguous blocks

The reported number of noncontiguous areas were found for that file.

filename File cluster number is invalid
[, entry truncated]

The file contains an invalid pointer. If you have used the /F option, the file will be truncated and the bracketed message will appear.

Insufficient room in root directory
Erase files from root and repeat CHKDSK

There is not enough room to convert lost blocks to files.

Invalid current directory

An unrecoverable read error was located on the disk; no action is required.

path Convert directory to file (Y/N)?

The directory has been determined to be no longer usable. Respond Y to convert it to a file.

path Invalid subdirectory

The subdirectory contains invalid information. CHKDSK attempts to correct the error. Use the /V option for more information.

Probable non-DOS disk.
Continue (Y/N)?

Either the disk being checked is not formatted properly or it is badly damaged. If you have not specified the /F option, responding Y tells CHKDSK to indicate corrective actions but not to perform them.

Processing cannot continue,

This message is followed by another message that indicates the reason CHKDSK is unable to continue.

Tree past this point not
processed

Track 0 on the disk is bad, so the path past the directory that is currently being checked could not continue.

Unrecoverable error on directory

An error was encountered in the directory; no action is required.

xxxxxxxxx bytes disk space freed

The indicated number of bytes of disk space was not allocated and therefore was freed.

***xxx* lost clusters found in *yyy* chains**

The indicated number of lost data blocks were not associated with any file.

NOTES

Running CHKDSK with the /F option can result in losing some information, so you should first run CHKDSK without the /F option. If CHKDSK reports errors, use the COPY command to copy the files off the disk as backup; then run CHKDSK /F. If you specify a file name or use the wildcard pattern *.*, CHKDSK reports the number of noncontiguous areas that the file(s) occupy on the disk. Version 1.0 of the command did not report available disk space, hidden files, user files, and bad sectors. It automatically ran with the /F option, fixing the disk while checking it.

SEE ALSO

BACKUP
COPY
DEBUG
FORMAT
TYPE

CLS

Clearing the Screen

Clears the screen.

VERSION

PC-DOS 2.0 +
MS-DOS equivalent: **CLS** (3.0 +)

TYPE

Internal

SYNTAX

CLS

EXAMPLE

CLS

BEFORE: Screen displays DOS commands that have been previously used.
AFTER: A blank screen displays only the DOS prompt.

COMMAND
Invoking a Second Command Processor

Invokes a second command processor.

PC-DOS 2.0+
MS-DOS equivalent: **COMMAND** (2.0+)

External

COMMAND [*d*]:[*path*][/P][/C *string*][/E:*xxxxx*]

d:path   Specifies the drive letter and path that is searched to locate the command processor you wish to start.

/P   Causes a second command processor to become memory-resident; you must then restart DOS to return to the original command processor.

/C *string*   Passes a string (any command that can be entered at a DOS prompt) to a second command processor, executes the command, and then removes the second copy of the command processor.

/E:*xxxxx*   Specifies the size of the environment as a base 10 integer between 160 and 32768. This number is rounded up to the nearest paragraph boundary.

COMMAND allows you to run one batch file from within another and then return to the original batch file.

EXAMPLES

C>COMMAND

invokes a second copy of the command processor, and this new copy will inherit the environment known to the primary command processor.

C>COMMAND /C TEST2

starts a second copy of the command processor and executes the batch file TEST2.BAT, then returns to the original batch file TEST1.BAT.

MESSAGE

Current drive is no longer valid

COMMAND found that the current drive is no longer valid. You may have deleted a network drive. Change the current drive to a valid one.

UNDO

To return to the primary command processor, enter the special command

C>EXIT

SEE ALSO

SET
Appendix A: Batch Files

COMP
Comparing Files

Compares the contents of two files.

VERSION

PC-DOS 2.0 + (revised from 1.0)
MS-DOS equivalent: **FILCOM** (2.0 +); **COMP** (1.0)

TYPE

External

SYNTAX

[*d:*][*path*] **COMP** [*pd:*][*ppath*][*pfilename*]
[*sd:*][*spath*][*sfilename*]

OPTIONS

d:path	Specifies the drive letter and path that contain the COMP command file.
pd:ppath *pfilename*	Specifies the first file or set of files that you wish to compare (*primary* file).
sd:spath *sfilename*	Specifies the second file or set of files that you wish to compare (*secondary* file).

COMP allows you to see whether two files are identical, such as comparing a file to its backed-up version saved under a different name.

EXAMPLE

COMP   B:TEST.TXT   C:TEST.TXT

compares the TEST.TXT file on drive B with the TEST.TXT file
on drive C.

MESSAGES

Compare error at offset *XXXXXXXX*
File 1 = *YY*
File 2 = *ZZ*

The *XXXXXXXX*th byte in the first file does not match the corres-
ponding byte in the second file. The two bytes (*XX* and *ZZ*) are displayed in hexadecimal notation.

Compare more files (Y/N)?

Enter Y to compare additional files.

EOF mark not found

COMP could not find the end of valid data. Many text files do not
end with Ctrl-Z. The message may be innocuous.

Files are different sizes.

COMP will only compare files that are of the same size.

File sharing conflict

One of the files that is being compared is currently being used by
another process. Try again later.

10 Mismatches—ending compare

Ten mismatched locations were found in the compared files.

NOTES

Version 2 allows you to use the *.* wildcard pattern to check all of
the files on a disk. DISKCOMP is faster for comparing two disks,

however. In many versions of MS-DOS, the command FILCOMP
provides additional information about how files differ. See the
appropriate user's manual for manufacturer-specific alternatives.

SEE ALSO

DISKCOMP

COPY

Copying Files

Copies, renames, and concatenates (combines) files.

VERSION

PC-DOS 2.0 + (revised from 1.0)
MS-DOS equivalent: **COPY** (2.0 +)

TYPE

Internal

SYNTAX

To copy files with the same or different names:

COPY **[/A][/B]** *[sd:][spath]sfilename* **[/A][/B]**
[td:][tpath]tfilename **[/A][/B][/V]**

To copy and combine files:

COPY **[/A][/B]** *[sd:][spath]sfilename* **[/A][/B]**
[+ *[cd:][cpath]cfilename* **[/A][/B]** . . .**]**
[td:][tpath]tfilename **[/A][/B][/V]**

OPTIONS

/A or /B   Indicates whether the preceding file and all
subsequent files are to be read as *ASCII* (text) or
binary files, and it is in effect until further
modified.

sd:spath *sfilename*	Specifies source file or files to be copied.
(source)/A	Causes the file to be treated as a text (ASCII) file (read only to the ^ Z mark).
(source)/B	Causes the entire file to be copied based on the size indicated in the directory (as a binary file).
td:tpath *tfilename*	Specifies target file or files to be copied to. The *tfilename* is specified if you wish to rename the target file during copy.
(target)/A	Adds a ^ Z (end of file) as the last character in an ASCII file.
(target)/B	Causes no ^ Z to be added to the end of a binary target file.
+ *cd:cpath* *cfilename*	Specifies file(s) to be combined with source file during copy.
/V	Tells DOS to verify that the target file is correct.

COPY is used to make copies from one disk to another, to duplicate a file on the same disk, to read or write to or from external devices, and to combine files.

EXAMPLES

COPY   C:\TEST.FIL   C:\DOS

copies TEST.FIL from the root directory to the subdirectory named DOS (if this subdirectory exists).

COPY   C:\TEST.FIL   C:\DOS\NEW.FIL

copies TEST.FIL from the root directory into the subdirectory DOS, naming the copy NEW.FIL.

COPY   A:*.*   B:

copies all the files from the current directory on the disk in drive A to a disk in drive B, using their same file names.

COPY   TEST.FIL   COM1

sends the contents of TEST.FIL to COM1.

COPY   CON: QUICK.FIL

sends whatever you type at the keyboard to a file named QUICK-
.FIL. To end the file, press Ctrl-Z and Return.

COPY   TEST.FIL + NEW.FIL   TEST2.FIL

concatenates TEST.FIL and NEW.FIL into TEST2.FIL.

COPY   TEST.FIL + NEW.FIL

concatenates TEST.FIL and NEW.FIL under the name TEST.FIL.

COPY   TEST.FIL   TEST2.FIL   /V

makes another copy of TEST.FIL under the name TEST2.FIL, and
verifies that the copy is correct.

MESSAGES

Cannot do binary reads from a device

The /B option was used while attempting to copy from a system
device. Omit the /B and retry.

File cannot be copied onto itself

You tried to make a copy of a file on the same disk without changing
its name. Specify a new file name and retry.

File not found

The file does not exist or there is an error in the way its name was
typed.

Invalid path or name

The path or file name that was specified does not exist.

| UNDO |

Repeat the COPY command using correct drive/directory and/or file name parameters. If you renamed the file during the copy, be sure to use the new file name when repeating the COPY command. Also, delete the unwanted copy.

| NOTES |

If a target file name is not specified, the source file name is used. If there is more than one source file, as in a concatenation, the name of the first source file is used. Wildcards may be used. Device names may be used in place of file names.

The /A and /B options are seldom used; when they are, it is to distinguish between ASCII (text) and binary files that contain special nontext characters, such as program files and database files. When concatenating files, /A is the default; otherwise, /B is the default.

CTTY
Changing to a Remote Terminal

Specifies that a remote terminal will be used instead of the primary
keyboard and screen.

VERSION

PC-DOS 2.0+
MS-DOS equivalent: **CTTY** (2.0+)

TYPE

Internal

SYNTAX

CTTY *devicename*

OPTIONS

devicename   Specifies AUX, COM1, COM2, COM3, or
COM4 to be used as the primary console.

CTTY is used to connect a terminal to a communications port so
that it can be used as a secondary terminal.

EXAMPLE

CTTY COM1

redirects input and output to the COM1 port.

MESSAGE

Invalid device

DOS does not recognize the device name you specified. Reissue the command, using a valid device name.

UNDO

After you have switched the console to another port, you must use the new console to switch back to the regular console by giving the command

CTTY CON

If the new terminal is not set at the correct baud rate and protocol, you may have to reboot to use the regular terminal again.

DATE

Entering the Current Date

Displays the current system date; allows you to enter a new date.

VERSION

PC-DOS 2.0 + (revised from 1.1; revised again in PC-DOS 3.3)
MS-DOS equivalent: **DATE** (2.0 +)

TYPE

Internal

SYNTAX

DATE   [*mm-dd-yy*]

or

DATE   [*mm/dd/yy*]

or

DATE   [*yy-mm-dd*]

DATE allows you to reset the system date to the current date or obtain the current date from the system clock.

EXAMPLES

DATE   1-1-88

sets the system date to Fri 1-01-1988. You may separate day, month, and year with hyphens (-), slashes (/), or periods (.). You do not need to type leading zeros.

DATE

returns the current date and prompts you for a new one.

MESSAGE

Invalid date

The date you entered used an invalid format. Check your entry and try again.

UNDO

To reset the date, type

DATE

and enter the current date in one of the allowable formats.

NOTES

In version 3.3 of PC-DOS, if your computer has an internal clock, the DATE command also resets it. (This is the inverse of previous versions.) You can include the DATE command in an AUTO-EXEC.BAT file so that you are not prompted for the date when you boot DOS. If there is no clock that DOS can read, the prompts still come up. To change the date format, create a CONFIG.SYS file that includes the COUNTRY command.

SEE ALSO

Appendix A: Batch Files
Appendix B: The CONFIG.SYS File

DEL and ERASE
Deleting Files

Deletes files.

VERSION

PC-DOS 2.0+ (revised from 1.1)
MS-DOS equivalent: **DEL** and **ERASE** (2.0+)

TYPE

Internal

SYNTAX

ERASE   [*d:*][*path*]*filename*
DEL   [*d:*][*path*]*filename*

OPTIONS

*d:path
filename*   Specifies the file or group of files to be erased.

EXAMPLES

DEL   TEST.TXT

BEFORE: File directory lists MSTEST.TXT in current directory.
AFTER: File directory no longer lists MSTEST.TXT in current
directory.

ERASE   A:*.*

BEFORE: File directory lists all files created in current directory.
AFTER: File directory lists no files in current directory.

Note that when you use the global wildcard *.*, you will be prompted to confirm the deletion (see the MESSAGES that follow).

DEL   C:\WP\FILES*.CAP

BEFORE: File directory lists all files in directory C:\WP\FILES with the extension .CAP.
AFTER: File directory lists no files with the extension .CAP in directory C:\WP\FILES.

DEL   C:\WP

BEFORE: File directory lists all files in directory C:\WP.
AFTER: File directory lists no files in directory C:\WP.

MESSAGES

Are you sure (Y/N)?

You have specified *.* (all files regardless of extension). Enter Y to erase all files on the specified drive and directory; otherwise, enter N.

File not found

DOS was unable to locate the file(s) you specified. Check the path name and try again.

Invalid number of parameters

Check the path name and try again.

UNDO

You can restore files deleted with the DEL or ERASE command with a DOS utility such as the Norton Utilities or Mace Utilities, or by using the DOS DEBUG program.

NOTES

The DEL and ERASE commands are used to erase files, not directories. You may issue the command as DELETE, DEL, or ERASE. If no drive is specified, the current drive is assumed. If you specify a directory instead of a file, all files in that directory will be erased. You cannot delete files that have been marked as read-only. Versions of the command after version 1.0 require confirmations to prompts before erasing.

DIR

Listing Files in a Directory

Lists files contained in a directory.

VERSION

PC-DOS 2.0 + (revised from 1.1)
MS-DOS equivalent: **DIR** (2.0 +)

TYPE

Internal

SYNTAX

DIR [*d:*][*path*][*filename*] [/P][/W]

OPTIONS

d:path *filename*	Specify the drive letter, path name, or file name when you wish to obtain a directory listing of files that are not in the current directory.
/P	Tells DOS to pause when the screen has been filled. To see the next screen of file names, press any key.
/W	Displays a directory showing only file names in a wide format—five names across each line.

DIR is used to display the contents of a directory as well as the file size in bytes, the date and time of last modification, the number of bytes available on the disk, and any subdirectories under the current directory.

DIR   C:

displays the contents of the current working directory on drive C.

DIR   C:*.MAC

displays only those files in the current working directory of drive C that have the .MAC extension.

If you have used the /V option with the FORMAT command, the first line of the DIR listing will report the name of the disk label. If you did not label your disk, this line reads

Volume in drive *x* **has no label**

This information is not provided in early versions of the DIR command. The DIR command does not list hidden files that are created by the FORMAT and the SYS commands. The CHKDSK command lists these files. The /W and /P options affect only how the files are displayed (wide or with pauses between screenfuls), not the content of what is displayed on the screen.

CHKDSK
FORMAT
SYS

DISKCOMP
Comparing Disks

Compares disks.

VERSION

PC-DOS 2.0 + (revised from 1.1)
MS-DOS equivalent: **DISKCOMP** (2.0 +)

TYPE

External

SYNTAX

[*d:*][*path*]   **DISKCOMP**   [*sd:*   [*td:*]]   [/1][/8]

OPTIONS

d:path	Specifies the drive letter and path that contain the DISKCOMP command file.
sd:	Specifies the source drive letter.
sd:	Specifies the target drive letter.
/1	Compares only the first side of a two-sided disk.
/8	Specifies that only eight sectors per track are to be compared.

DISKCOMP is used to verify the readability of a disk, usually after a DISKCOPY operation.

EXAMPLES

DISKCOMP   A: B:

compares the disk in drive A with the disk in drive B.

DISKCOMP   A: A:

compares the disk in drive A to another disk that you will be prompted to insert in drive A.

MESSAGES

Compare error(s) on new line
Track *xx*, side *yy*

There is a discrepancy between the two compared disks on the track and side indicated.

Compare more diskettes (Y/N)?

Enter Y to compare another set of disks; otherwise, enter N.

Comparing *x* sectors per track, *n* side(s)

This message indicates whether one or two sides are being compared and whether eight or nine sectors are being compared.

Diskettes compare OK

Identical information is located in identical sectors on the two disks.

Diskette/Drive not compatible

The destination disk or drive is different from the source disk or drive. You may be trying to compare a double-sided disk to a single-sided disk, for example. Use the same type of disks and drives and try again.

Insert first diskette in drive *x*
Insert second diskette in drive *y*
Strike any key when ready

Insert the disks to be compared as specified. Then press any key.

Make sure a diskette is inserted into the drive and the door is closed

The drive door is open, or the drive is empty. Close the door or insert a disk and try again.

Specified drive does not exist, or is non-removable

The drive you specified is a hard disk or does not exist on your computer. Check the drive name and try again.

Unrecoverable read error in drive *x* Track *yy*, side *z*

The unreadable data is located on the track and side indicated.

| NOTES | 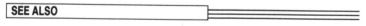 |

Version 1.0 does not work with two-sided drives. Later versions work with nine sectors per track. DISKCOMP compares all 40 tracks on a track-by-track basis and issues an error message if any tracks do not match. If an error is located, the comparison operation ends, indicating that you should probably make a new copy of the disk. Only similar disks may be compared: single-sided to single-sided, or double-sided to double-sided. The drives used with DISK-COMP cannot be virtual disks, such as one created by using the SUBST command. In addition, do not use DISKCOMP when the JOIN command is in effect.

| SEE ALSO |

DISKCOPY

DISKCOPY
Copying Disks

Copies disks; optionally formats the target disk also.

VERSION

PC-DOS 2.0 + (revised from 1.1)
MS-DOS equivalent: **DISKCOPY** (2.0 +)

TYPE

External

SYNTAX

[*d:*][*path*]   **DISKCOPY**   [*sd:*   [*td:*]]   [**/1**]

OPTIONS

d:path	Specifies the drive letter and path that contain the DISKCOPY command file.
sd:	Specifies the source drive letter.
td:	Specifies the target drive letter.
/1	Copies only the first side of a double-sided disk.

EXAMPLES

DISKCOPY   A: B:

copies the disk in drive A onto the disk in drive B.

DISKCOPY A: A:

copies the disk in drive A to another disk that you will be prompted to insert in drive A.

DISKCOPY B:

copies the disk in drive B to the disk in the default drive.

DISKCOPY

copies the disk in the default drive to another disk that will be placed in the default drive.

MESSAGES

Copy complete

The source disk has been copied onto the target disk.

Copy another (Y/N)?

Enter Y to make another copy; otherwise, enter N.

Copying x sectors per track, n side(s)

This message indicates whether one or two sides are being copied and whether eight or nine sectors are being copied.

Diskette/Drive not compatible

The destination disk or drive is different from the source disk or drive. You may be trying to copy a double-sided disk to a single-sided disk, for example. Use the same type of disks and drives and try again.

Formatting while copying

The target disk is being formatted in the same format as the source disk.

Insert source diskette in drive x
Insert target diskette in drive y

Insert the appropriate disks in the correct drives.

Incompatible drive types

The first disk and drive are two-sided and the second drive or disk is one-sided. Use the /1 option.

Make sure a diskette is inserted into the drive and the door is closed

The drive door is open, or the drive is empty. Close the door or insert a disk and try again.

Source diskette bad or incompatible

There may be bad sectors in the source disk, or it may not be compatible with the drive. Check to make sure the disk is of the type that the drive accepts and try again, or try with a new disk.

Specified drive does not exist, or is non-removable

The drive you specified is a hard disk or does not exist on your computer. Check the drive name and try again.

Target diskette may be unusable

There is an unrecoverable read, write, or verify error on the target disk.

Target diskette unusable

The target disk is dirty or damaged, or the drive is not able to read all the tracks. Change the disk and try again.

Target write protected Correct, then strike any key

Insert another non–write-protected disk or remove the write-protection tab; then press any key to continue.

Unrecoverable format error on target Target diskette unusable

An unrecoverable error occurred; the target disk contains no usable data. Use a new disk and try again.

Unrecoverable read error on source
Track *xx*, side *yy*

Four unsuccessful attempts were made to read data at that location.
DISKCOPY will continue; however, the copy may not be complete.

Unrecoverable verify error on target
Track *xx*, side *yy*

Four unsuccessful attempts were made to verify data at that location.
DISKCOPY will continue; however, the copy may not be accurate.

Unrecoverable write error on target
Track *xx*, side *yy*

Four unsuccessful attempts were made to write data at that location.
DISKCOPY will continue; however, the copy may not be complete.

```
NOTES
```

Version 1.0 does not work with double-sided drives. Later versions
automatically check whether the source drive and disk are single- or
double-sided, and make the copy accordingly. Later versions work
with nine sectors per track. The drives used with DISKCOPY cannot be virtual disks, such as one created by using the SUBST command. In addition, do not use DISKCOPY when the JOIN
command is in effect. DISKCOPY is not recommended for use with
heavily used disks because it does not reduce fragmentation; use the
COPY command with such disks instead.

```
SEE ALSO
```

COPY
DISKCOMP
SUBST

ERASE

See DEL and ERASE.

EXE2BIN

Converting .EXE Files to .BIN Files

Converts an .EXE file to a .BIN file, which may be used as a .COM file by renaming it with the .COM extension if it is in .COM file format, or by giving a .COM extension to the second argument.

VERSION

PC-DOS 2.0 + (revised from 1.1; none in 1.0)
MS-DOS equivalent: **EXE2BIN** (2.0 +)

TYPE

External

SYNTAX

[*d:*][*path*] **EXE2BIN** [*sd:*][*spath*]*sfilename*
[*td:*][*tpath*]*tfilename*]

OPTIONS

d:path	Specifies the drive letter and path that contain the EXE2BIN command file.
sd:spath *sfilename*	Specifies the file name of the .EXE file to be converted.
td:tpath *tfilename*	Specifies the file name of the .BIN file to be created.

EXE2BIN is used to convert an .EXE (executable) file to a .BIN (binary) file, which is formatted for more efficient storage and operation.

EXAMPLE

EXE2BIN   TEST.FIL   TEST.COM

BEFORE: TEST.FIL
AFTER: TEST.COM

MESSAGES

Amount read less than size in header

The program portion of the .EXE file was less than the program
header indicates. Recompile or reassemble the program again; then
relink it before continuing.

Fixups needed—base segment (hex)

The source file indicates that a load segment is required. Specify the
absolute address at which the completed .COM file is to be loaded.

WARNING—Read error on EXE file

An error in reading the input file occurred. EXE2BIN will continue; however, the resulting file may not be executable.

NOTES

Only executable code that is completely relocatable in memory and
run at a specific memory location can be converted by this command. In addition, the memory image of the .EXE file must be less
than 64K. If you do not specify an output file name, the input file
name will be used.

FASTOPEN

Storing the Location of Files in Memory

Stores in memory the location of directories and recently opened files so that files can be located quickly.

VERSION

PC-DOS 3.3

TYPE

External

SYNTAX

[*d:*][*path*] **FASTOPEN** *pd:*[= *nnn*]

OPTIONS

d:path   Specifies the drive letter and path that contain the FASTOPEN command file.

pd: Specifies the drive to process.

= *nnn*   Specifies the number of directories or files to remember for the drive specified as *pd:*. If no number is specified, the default of 34 is used. The range of numbers specified must be between 10 and 999. In addition, the sum of all *nnn* files cannot exceed 999.

FASTOPEN is used to speed up access of files on hard disks with complex directory structures.

EXAMPLE ══════════════════

FASTOPEN   C:100

instructs DOS to remember the locations of the last 100 directories or files that were opened on drive C.

MESSAGES ══════════════════

Cannot use FASTOPEN for drive *x*

FASTOPEN can be used only on hard disk drives. It cannot be used on floppy drives or on network drives, or on drives that have been operated on with the JOIN, SUBST, or ASSIGN command.

FASTOPEN already installed

FASTOPEN has already been loaded. No action is required.

Same drive specified more than once

Reenter the command, specifying each drive letter once.

Too many drive entries

You have specified too many drive letters. Reenter the command with fewer drive letters.

Too many name entries

You have specified a number greater than 999. Change the number to less than 999 and try again.

NOTES ══════════════════

FASTOPEN is used only once, and it is usually placed in the AUTOEXEC.BAT file.

The minimum number of directories or file entries that FAST-OPEN remembers the location of is 10; the maximum is 999.

The number you assign should be greater than the deepest level of subdirectory you are using. If you access more than the number of files you specified during a session, the least recently accessed file is removed from the list and replaced by the most recently accessed file.

FDISK

Partitioning the Hard Disk

Serves as a menu-driven hard disk preparation program.

VERSION

PC-DOS 2.0 + (revised in 3.3)
MS-DOS equivalent: **FDISK**

TYPE

External

SYNTAX

[*d:*][*path*] **FDISK**

OPTIONS

d:path   Specifies the drive letter and path that contain
                the FDISK command file.

You will see the following options on the FDISK menu:

1   Create DOS Partition

2   Change Active Partition

3   Delete DOS Partition

4   Display Partition Data

5   Select Next Fixed Disk Drive

You must use the FDISK command each time you start up a new
hard disk. It establishes the physical area of the disk that is used by
DOS (partitions the disk).

MESSAGES

All logical drives deleted in the Extended DOS partition

No more logical drives are defined in the extended DOS partition. You can delete the extended DOS partition if you no longer need it for additional drives.

Cannot create extended DOS partition without primary DOS partition on disk 1

You cannot have an extended DOS partition on disk 1 unless you also have a primary DOS partition. Create a primary DOS partition using FDISK, and leave sufficient space for the extended partition.

Cannot delete extended DOS partition while logical drives exist

As long as logical drives are defined in an extended DOS partition, you cannot delete it. Use FDISK to delete all logical drives in the extended partition.

Cannot run FDISK with network loaded

You cannot run this command while the network program is loaded. Restart the machine and then run FDISK.

DOS partition already exists

DOS has already been set up on this hard disk.

Error reading fixed disk

FDISK was unable to read the hard disk. Reissue the FDISK command. If the error message persists, consult your IBM *Guide to Operations* (the Problem Determination section) or your dealer.

Extended DOS partition already exists

Use option 4 of the FDISK menu to display information about the partitions that are already on the hard disk.

No Extended DOS partition to delete

Use option 4 of the FDISK menu to display information about the partitions that are already on the hard disk.

No fixed disks present

Your system either does not have a hard disk, has a hard disk in an expansion unit that is not turned on, or has an improperly installed hard disk. Check to see that the expansion unit is turned on, or reinstall your hard disk.

No logical drives defined

There are no logical drives that have been defined in the extended DOS partition. Use FDISK to create a logical drive, and then format the newly created drive by using the FORMAT command.

No partitions defined

There are no partitions that have been defined in the extended DOS partition. Use FDISK to create a primary DOS partition, and then format the drive by using the FORMAT command.

No partitions to delete

Use option 4 of the FDISK menu to display information about the partitions that are already on the hard disk.

No partitions to make active

Use the Create DOS Partition option (1) to create a partition; then use the Change Active Partition option (2) to make it active.

No Primary DOS partition to delete

Use option 4 of the FDISK menu to display information about the partitions that are already on the hard disk.

No space for a *xxxx* cylinder partition

You have entered a cylinder size that is larger than the amount of free space. Enter a smaller number.

No space to create a DOS partition

Remove the existing partition or reduce its size. Then run FDISK again.

No space to create logical drive

Use FDISK to delete an existing logical drive; then run FDISK again to create the new logical drive.

Only non-bootable partitions exist

FDISK was requested to change the active partition, but none of the other partitions can boot from the hard disk. Create a bootable partition, such as the primary DOS partition.

Only partitions on Disk 1 can be made active

The system uses the first hard disk to boot from. Use the FDISK command to make a partition active so that the hard disk will boot the system.

Partition selected (#) is not bootable, active partition not changed

Use FDISK to select a bootable partition to be active.

Primary DOS partition already exists

You can have only one primary DOS partition on a hard disk. Use option 4 on the FDISK menu to display information about the partitions that are already on the hard disk.

NOTES

With FDISK you can choose to use the entire disk for DOS, or you can allocate space on the hard disk to other operating systems. In version 3.3 of PC-DOS you can also create extended DOS partitions that can be further subdivided into logical drives, such as drives D and E.

After you have used the FDISK command, use the SELECT command to format the hard disk, copy the DOS commands from the DOS disk to the hard disk, and specify the keyboard layout and date/time formats you want to use. You can then boot directly from the hard disk. (Alternatively, you can format the disk with the FORMAT C:/S/V command to transfer the system files and give a volume label; then use the COPY command to copy the DOS commands from the DOS floppy disk.)

If you are creating multiple partitions, you will be prompted to specify the size of the partition; press Return to accept the default, or enter any number that is less than the maximum cylinder size you will see displayed at the bottom of the screen. Likewise, when you are prompted for a starting cylinder number, press Return for the default, or enter a cylinder number based on the information displayed on the screen. For example, if you chose 25 cylinders less than the maximum, you can start the partition 25 cylinders further from the starting number on the screen.

If you are creating multiple partitions and wish to make the one you just created the active partition, you must select option 2. Option 3 deletes the DOS partition. If you select it, you will be prompted through a process that deletes the DOS partition along with all data files and programs it contains. Option 4 allows you to view the status of the partitions that exist on the hard disk. Option 5 is designed to be used if you have a second hard disk. It allows you to switch to that drive to perform FDISK operations.

SEE ALSO ===============================

FORMAT
SELECT

FILCOM

See COMP.

FIND

Finding Strings within Files

Locates and displays all lines in a file or group of files that contain a specified string.

VERSION

PC-DOS 2.0+
MS-DOS equivalent: **FIND** (2.0+)

TYPE

External

SYNTAX

[*d:*][*path*] **FIND** [/V][/C][/N] *"string"*
[*sd:*][*spath*]*sfilename*

OPTIONS
---

d:path	Specifies the drive letter and path that contain the FIND command file.
/V	Displays all lines that do not contain the string.
/C	Displays a count of the lines that contain the string.
/N	Displays the line number of each line found as well as the line.
"string"	Specifies the search string, which can have up to 250 characters and must be enclosed in double quotes. Wildcards are not permitted.

sd:spath	Specifies the file to be searched. FIND locates
sfilename	all records or lines in the file that match the
	specified search string.

EXAMPLES

FIND   "Oct. 28, 1988"   INVOICES.TXT

locates and displays all lines containing the string "Oct. 28, 1988" in the file named INVOICES.TXT.

FIND   "Oct. 28, 1988"   INVOICES.TXT   B:STMNTS.TXT

locates and displays all lines containing the string "Oct. 28, 1988" in the file named INVOICES.TXT on the default drive and the file named STMNTS.TXT on drive B.

FIND   /V/C"Oct. 28, 1988"   INVOICES.TXT

returns

– – – – – INVOICES.TXT: 201

indicating that 201 lines in the file did not contain the string.

FIND   "Smith"   INVOICES.TXT FIND "Reno"

locates all of the lines in INVOICES.TXT that contain Smith. Then, it passes this information to the FIND filter a second time to locate all of the lines that also contain the city Reno. The resulting output will display only those lines that contain both Smith and Reno.

NOTES

Used with the MORE command, the output from FIND can be sent to the screen one screen at a time.

SEE ALSO

MORE

FORMAT
Formatting Disks

Prepares a disk by rearranging random magnetic impulses into a series of tracks and sectors so that it is addressable by DOS.

VERSION

PC-DOS 2.0 + (revised from 1.0)
MS-DOS equivalent: **FORMAT** (2.0 +)

TYPE

External

SYNTAX

[*d:*][*path*]   **FORMAT**   *fd:*[/S][/1][/8][/V][/B][/4][/N:*xx*][/T:*yy*]

OPTIONS

d:path	Specifies the drive letter and path that contain the FORMAT command file.
fd:	Specifies the disk to be formatted.
/S	Transfers DOS files to the disk being formatted.
/1	Formats only one side of a double-sided disk.
/8	Formats eight sectors per track instead of nine (not for hard disks).
/V	Writes a volume label on the disk. Cannot be used with the /8 option.

/B	Creates an eight sector per track disk and reserves space for DOS without transferring it.
/4	Formats a single- or double-sided disk in a 1.2-megabyte high-capacity drive.
/N:xx	Allows you to specify the number of sectors per track to format.
/T:yy	Allows you to specify the number of tracks to format.

EXAMPLES

FORMAT B:

formats the disk in drive B.

FORMAT B:/S

places the DOS files on the disk in drive B as it formats it, which makes the disk a system disk. To make the disk bootable as well, copy COMMAND.COM onto it.

FORMAT B:/V

writes a volume label on the disk being formatted. You will be prompted to enter a label. You can enter up to 11 characters.

FORMAT B:/1

formats the disk in drive B as a single-sided disk. For example, you may be using a double-sided floppy drive but want to format a disk so that it can be read by a single-sided drive.

FORMAT A:/1/8

formats the disk in drive A as a single-sided disk, eight sectors per track. This makes the disk readable by a single-sided drive using version 1 of DOS.

FORMAT   A:/B

formats the disk in drive A without actually transferring DOS to the disk but leaving room for it. You must use the SYS command to write the system files on a disk formatted with the /B option.

MESSAGES

Attempted write protect violation

The disk you are trying to format is write-protected. Remove the write-protection or insert a new disk.

Bad Partition Table

The hard disk does not have a DOS partition, or the partition table is invalid. Use FDISK to set up a new DOS partition and then retry FORMAT.

Cannot find system files

The hidden files IBMBIO.COM and IBMDOS.COM could not be located on the hard disk. Change to a drive that contains the system files and try again.

Cannot FORMAT a Network drive

You cannot use the FORMAT command to format a network drive or a drive on a computer that is being shared on a network. If your computer is being shared, have the server pause and then issue the FORMAT command.

Cannot format an ASSIGNed or SUBSTed drive

You cannot format a drive after an ASSIGN or SUBST command has been used to reassign its designation. Issue the ASSIGN command to restore the original drive assignments; then reissue the FORMAT command.

Disk not compatible

The drive you specified is not supported by the IBM device interfaces required by the FORMAT command. Use a different disk drive.

Disk unsuitable for system disk

There is a defective track in the area that contains the DOS files. Use this disk only for data; use a different disk to contain DOS files.

Drive letter must be specified

Reissue the command with the drive letter of the disk to be formatted.

Error reading partition table

A hardware error probably occurred. Reissue the FORMAT command.

Error writing partition table

A hardware error probably occurred. Reissue the FORMAT command.

Format failure

The disk is unusable. Reissue the FORMAT command using another disk.

Format not supported on drive *n:*

The disk device driver cannot handle certain calls. If you have replaced the default disk device driver, remove it from your CONFIG.SYS file and try again. If not, reinstall DOS on your boot disk and try the FORMAT command again.

Invalid characters in volume label

You have used characters that are not valid. Retry, using valid characters.

Invalid device parameters from device driver

The number of hidden sectors is not a multiple of the number of sectors per track. Set up a new DOS partition by using FDISK; then reissue the FORMAT command.

Invalid media or track 0 bad - disk unusable

Either track 0 is bad, in which case the disk is unusable, or the disk and the drive are incompatible. Check the disk and drive; if they are incompatible types, reissue FORMAT with the /4 option. If they are compatible, use a new disk.

Parameter not compatible with fixed disk

You used the /1 or /8 options, neither of which can be used with a hard disk. Reissue the command with the correct options.

Unable to write BOOT

The first track of the disk or the DOS partition is bad; the disk is unusable. Get a different disk and try again.

UNDO

If you format a disk that contained files you wish to retain, you can use the Mace Utilities UnFORMAT command to restore them, unless you are using a version of Compaq MS-DOS, AT&T MS-DOS prior to version 3.1, or Burroughs MS-DOS.

NOTES

No data can be stored on an unformatted disk. When a disk is formatted, any data on it is erased. Version 2.0 + works with a hard disk, formats nine sectors per track, and accepts a volume label. Version 1.0 does not work with a hard disk. To avoid inadvertently formatting a hard disk, thus erasing any and all data on it, you can rename the FORMAT command and create a batch file that gives you warning prompts when you use this command.

SEE ALSO

FDISK
DISKCOPY
RENAME

GRAFTABL
Loading Graphics Characters

Loads graphics characters with ASCII codes greater than 127 so that they can be used with the color/graphics adapter.

VERSION

PC-DOS 3.0+
MS-DOS equivalent: **GRAFTABL** (3.0+)

TYPE

External

SYNTAX

[*d:*][*path*]   **GRAFTABL**   [*nnn*][**/STATUS**]

OPTIONS

d:path   Specifies the drive letter and path that contain the GRAFTABL command file.

nnn   Specifies the country code page according to the following values:

                437   United States (default)

                860   Portugal

                863   Canada (French)

                865   Norway and Denmark

/STATUS   Displays the number of the current country code page.

EXAMPLE

GRAFTABL   863

loads the table of graphics characters for the Canadian (French) code page. ASCII characters 128 through 255 will now be displayed in the graphics mode if the system has a color/graphics adapter.

MESSAGES

Incorrect parameter

An unidentifiable parameter was specified. Check the parameters and retry.

No version of Graphic Character Set Table is already loaded

GRAFTABL has not been used to load character tables; no action is required.

Non-Standard version of Graphics Character Set Table is already loaded

A previously loaded character set table has been modified; no action is required.

nnn version of Graphic Character Set Table is now loaded

The code page numbered *nnn* has been loaded; no further action is required.

NOTES

When this command has been executed, it increases the size of DOS by 1296 bytes. GRAFTABL may be used multiple times to change the loaded graphics characters.

GRAPHICS

Printing a Graphics Screen

Allows the contents of a graphics screen to be printed on an IBM graphics or compatible printer.

VERSION

PC-DOS 2.0+
MS-DOS equivalent: **GRAPHICS** (3.0+)

TYPE

External

SYNTAX

[*d:*][*path*]   **GRAPHICS**   [*printertype*]   [/R][/B][/LCD]

OPTIONS

d:path	Specifies the drive letter and path that contain the GRAPHICS command file.
printertype	Specifies the type of printer you are using from among the following types:

COLOR1	IBM PC Color Printer with black ribbon
COLOR4	IBM PC Color Printer with RGB ribbon
COLOR8	IBM PC Color Printer with CMY ribbon

COMPACT	IBM PC Compact Printer
GRAPHICS	IBM Personal Graphics Printer or IBM Proprinter
THERMAL	IBM PC Convertible Printer

/R — Prints black and white on the page as they are displayed on the screen. If you do not use the /R parameter, black will print as white and white will print as black.

/B — Prints background color. Use only for printer types COLOR4 or COLOR8. If you do not use the /B parameter with these printers, the background color will not be printed.

/LCD — Prints image exactly as it appears on the IBM PC Convertible Liquid Crystal Display.

EXAMPLE

GRAPHICS   COLOR4   /B/R

loads the graphics support for the IBM PC Color Printer with RGB (red, green, blue, and black) ribbon. It also prints the background color and black as black, and prints white as white.

UNDO

To undo the GRAPHICS command, reboot the computer with Ctrl-Alt-Del.

NOTES

Once this command has been executed, pressing Shift-PrtSc causes the contents of the screen to be printed out. It requires not only a printer with graphics capability but also a color/graphics monitor adapter. It increases the resident size of DOS by 688 bytes.

JOIN
Joining Drives to a Directory

Joins a drive to a subdirectory of another drive.

VERSION

PC-DOS 2.0+
MS-DOS equivalent: **JOIN** (3.0+)

TYPE

External

SYNTAX

[*d:*][*path*]   **JOIN**   *sd:*   *td:\directory*

or

[*d:*][*path*]   **JOIN**   *td:***/D**

OPTIONS

d:path	Specifies the drive letter and path that contain the JOIN command file.
sd:	Specifies the source drive to be joined to a directory on another drive.
td:\directory	Specifies the target directory you will join a drive under.
/D	Disconnects the join. You must specify the drive letter of the drive whose join you are deleting.

JOIN is used to run programs that understand only floppy disks on a hard disk system.

JOIN   C: B:\HARDISK

makes files on drive C accessible by referencing them through the subdirectory named HARDISK on drive B.

JOIN

displays all currently existing JOINs.

Cannot JOIN to a network drive

The JOIN command will not join local and network drives.

Directory not empty

You have tried to use JOIN on a directory that is not empty. The directory must be empty. Reenter the command using an empty directory.

Invalid parameter

You have tried to use JOIN on the current directory. Reenter the directory path using a noncurrent directory.

Invalid drive specification

You have tried to refer to a joined drive. Disconnect the join using the /D parameter.

Issue the command

JOIN   *d:*   /D

where *d:* is the drive letter of the drive whose join you wish to delete.

NOTES

The directory you specify cannot be the root directory (\). The directory being joined to must be empty. Do not use JOIN with ASSIGN or SUBST. Do not use BACKUP, RESTORE, FORMAT, DISKCOPY, or DISKCOMP while a JOIN is in effect.

SEE ALSO

ASSIGN
SUBST

KEYB   3.3

Loading Foreign Keyboards [PC-DOS]

Used in version 3.3 of PC-DOS to load non–U.S.-English keyboards.

VERSION

PC-DOS 3.3

TYPE

External

SYNTAX

[*d:*][*path*]   **KEYB**   *xx,yyy*   [*sd:*][*spath*]**[KEYBOARD.SYS]**

OPTIONS

d:path   Specifies the drive letter and path that contain the KEYB command file.

xx   Specifies the keyboard code.

yyy   Specifies the code page that contains the character set you want to use. With no options, the KEYB command returns the status of the keyboard being used. Codes are as shown in the following table:

Country	Keyboard Code	Code Page
Arabic-language		785
Australia	US	061
Belgium	BE	032
Canada (Eng.)	US	001
Canada (Fr.)	CF	002
Denmark	DK	045
Finland	SU	358
France	FR	033
Germany	GR	049
Hebrew		972
Italy	IT	039
Latin America	LA	003
Netherlands	NL	031
Norway	NO	047
Portugal	PO	351
Spain	SP	034
Sweden	SV	046
Switzerland (Fr.)	SF	041
Switzerland (Gr.)	SG	041
United Kingdom	UK	044
United States	US	001

sd:spath KEYBOARD .SYS   Specifies the source drive letter and path of the KEYBOARD.SYS file if this file is not located in the current directory.

KEYB   SV,046

loads the Swedish keyboard's character set.

KEYB

returns the code for the type of keyboard that is being used.

Active codepage not available from CON device

Either the code page switching CON driver has not been installed, or there is no CON code page currently loaded.

Bad or missing Keyboard Definition file

The KEYBOARD.SYS file either could not be located or contains invalid data. Copy a new KEYBOARD.SYS file from the original DOS start-up disk.

Codepage specified has not been designated

The code page you specified has not been prepared for your keyboard. Use the MODE command to prepare your CON (keyboard) device.

Codepage yyy is not valid for given keyboard code

Use the MODE command to change to a valid code page, or specify a valid code page with the KEYB command.

Codepage specified is inconsistent with invoked codepage

You have used a code page number that is not the currently invoked code page. Use the MODE command to change the code page to match your keyboard code page, or the characters you type may be displayed incorrectly.

Codepage specified is inconsistent with selected codepage

You have used a code page number that is not the currently selected code page. Use the MODE command to change the code page to match your keyboard code page, or the characters you type may be displayed incorrectly.

Codepage specified has not been prepared

Use the MODE command to prepare your keyboard device driver with the code page you want to use.

Invalid codepage specified

You have used invalid parameters in the KEYB command line. Check and try again.

Invalid keyboard specified

You have used invalid parameters in the KEYB command line. Check and try again.

Invalid syntax

You have used invalid parameters in the KEYB command line. Check and try again.

KEYB has not been installed

You used the KEYB command to query which keyboard is currently being used. You need to install the KEYB function.

Unable to create KEYB table in resident memory

The configuration you requested exceeds the amount of resident memory originally specified. Restart DOS and reinstall KEYB with a new configuration.

UNDO

You can switch from the keyboard loaded with KEYB to the U.S. English keyboard by pressing Ctrl-Alt-F1. Press Ctrl-Alt-F2 to return to the non–U.S. keyboard.

NOTES

To use "front-face" characters (those that are displayed on the front edge of certain keys), press and hold Ctrl-Alt while pressing the key. (If you are using a Canadian French keyboard, press and hold Alt-Shift instead.)

SEE ALSO

MODE

KEYB*xx*
Loading Foreign Keyboards

Loads a keyboard program that supports non–U.S. keyboards.

VERSION

PC-DOS 3.0 + (replaced by KEYB in PC-DOS 3.3)
MS-DOS equivalent: **KEYB*xx*** (3.0 +)

TYPE

External

SYNTAX

[*d:*][*path*]   **KEYB*xx***

OPTIONS

d:path   Specifies the drive and path that contain the KEYB command file.

xx   Specifies the two-letter code of the keyboard program to be used. You can choose from the following keyboard codes:

GR   Germany

FR   France

IT   Italy

SP   Spain

UK   United Kingdom

EXAMPLES

KEYBGR

loads German keyboard support.

KEYBUK

loads United Kingdom keyboard support.

UNDO

Ctrl-Alt-F1 returns you to the U.S.-English keyboard. Ctrl-Alt-F2 reactivates the keyboard selected with KEYB*xx*.

NOTES

This command allows you to create accented characters in the languages available. If you are using PC-DOS version 3.3, use the KEYB command.

SEE ALSO

KEYB

LABEL
Adding Volume Labels

Allows you to modify, add, or delete a volume label.

VERSION

PC-DOS 3.0 +
MS-DOS equivalent: **LABEL** (3.0 +)

TYPE

External

SYNTAX

[*d:*][*path*]   **LABEL**   [*ld:*][*volumelabel*]

OPTIONS

d:path	Specifies the drive letter and path that contain the LABEL command file.
ld:	Specifies the drive letter of the disk you wish to label.
volumelabel	Specifies the label to be used to identify the disk. The volume label can contain up to 11 characters.

EXAMPLE

LABEL   B:OCTSTMTS
labels the disk in drive B as OCTSTMTS.

MESSAGE

Cannot LABEL a Network drive

You cannot change an existing volume label or create a new one for a network drive.

NOTES

If you do not specify a label with the command, you will be prompted for the label or for whether you want the existing label to be deleted:

Volume in drive *x* **is** *xxxxxxxxxxx*
Volume label (11 characters, ENTER for none)?

MKDIR (MD)
Creating New Subdirectories

Creates a new subdirectory.

VERSION

PC-DOS 2.0 +
MS-DOS equivalent: **MKDIR (MD)** (2.0 +)

TYPE

Internal

SYNTAX

MD   [*d:*]*path*

OPTIONS

d: Specifies drive letter of disk you wish to create
the subdirectory on.

path   Specifies path of directory names, including
the name of the subdirectory to be created.
The entire path name must not exceed 63
characters, including backslashes.

EXAMPLES

MD   PHONES

creates a subdirectory named PHONES under your current subdirectory.

MD   B:PHONES

creates a new subdirectory under the default directory on the disk in drive B.

MD   \WP\FILES\PHONES

creates a new subdirectory named PHONES under the subdirectory FILES, which is under the subdirectory WP, which in turn is directly under the root directory (indicated by \).

UNDO

To delete a subdirectory that you have created with the MKDIR command, you must use the RMDIR (RD) command. Note that the subdirectory to be deleted with this command must be empty.

SEE ALSO

RMDIR (RD)

MODE

Setting Device Modes

Sets the mode of operation for a printer or color graphics display. In PC-DOS version 3.3, also controls code page switching and additional communications devices.

VERSION

PC-DOS 2.0 + (revised from 1.0; revised again in 3.3)
MS-DOS equivalent: **MODE** (2.0 +)

TYPE

External

SYNTAX (All Versions)

[*d:*][*path*]   **MODE**   **LPT#**[**:**][*n*][**,**[*m*][**,P**]]

or

[*d:*][*path*]   **MODE**   *n*

or

[*d:*][*path*]   **MODE**   [*display*]**,***shift*[**,T**]

or

[*d:*][*path*]   **MODE**   **COM#**[**:**]*baud*
[**,**[*parity*][**,**[*databits*][**,**[*stopbits*][**,P**]]]]

or

[*d:*][*path*]   **MODE**   **LPT#**[**:**] = **COM#**

| SYNTAX (Version 3.3 Only) | |

[d:][path] **MODE** device **CODEPAGE**
PREPARE = ((cplist) [cd:][cpath]cfilename)

or

[d:][path] **MODE** device **CODEPAGE** **SELECT** = cp

or

[d:][path] **MODE** device **CODEPAGE[**/STATUS**]**

or

[d:][path] **MODE** device **CODEPAGE** **REFRESH**

| OPTIONS | |

d:path	Specifies the drive letter and path that contain the MODE command file.
LPT#	In LPT#, # is the printer number (1, 2, or 3).
COM#	In COM#, # is the asynchronous communications adapter: 1 or 2 for all versions; 1, 2, 3, or 4 for PC-DOS version 3.3.
n	80 or 132 (characters per line for printer).
display	BW40, BW80, CO40, CO80, or MONO (for color graphics display).
m	6 or 8 (lines per inch of vertical spacing for printer).
shift	R or L (to shift display right and left for color graphics monitor).
P	Performs continuous retry when error detected.
T	Displays test pattern.
baud	110, 150, 300, 600, 1200, 2400, 4800, or 9600 (all versions); or 19,200 for PC-DOS 3.3.
parity	N (none), O (odd), or E (even—default).
databits	7 (default) or 8.

stopbits	1 or 2 (if baud rate is 110, 2 is default; if baud rate other than 110, default is 1).
device	CON, PRN, LPT1, LPT2, or LPT3.
cp	Specifies one code page number: 437, 850, 860, 863, or 865.
cplist	Specifies one or more code page numbers, which are separated by commas, and the list is enclosed in parentheses. Must be selected from the following values: 437, 850, 860, 863, or 865.
cd:cpath cfilename	Specifies the file that contains the code pages. Choose from the following files:

4201.CPI	IBM Proprinter
5202.CPI	IBM Quietwriter III Printer
EGA.CPI	EGA-type devices
LCD.CPI	IBM Convertible LCD

MODE is used to change the way DOS communicates with hardware using different protocols, such as printers, display units, and modems. It is also used to specify different character sets (code pages) for use with various keyboards and printers in PC-DOS version 3.3.

EXAMPLES

MODE LPT1: 132,8,P

sets the IBM-compatible printer connected to LPT1 to 132 characters per line and 8 lines per inch (condensed). The P specifies that DOS should continuously attempt to send data to the port.

MODE CO80

switches from the monochrome to the color adapter and sets it to 80 characters across.

MODE 40

switches the color adapter to 40-column mode (you cannot use 40-column mode on the monochrome adapter).

MODE   MONO

switches to the monochrome adapter.

MODE   80,L,T

moves the color display left, and tests to see whether it is centered by displaying a test pattern.

MODE   COM1:   9600,N,8,1

sets the communications port COM1 to 9600 baud, no parity, 8 data bits, and 1 stop bit.

MODE   LPT1: = COM1

sends the output normally sent to LPT1 (the parallel port) to COM1 (the serial port).

MESSAGES

Codepage not prepared

MODE failed during a SELECT operation either because the indicated code page was never defined for the device or because the code pages that have been prepared do not have the proper font for the current video mode. Use MODE PREPARE to prepare the device with the code page. If an error message still appears, increase the number of fonts in the DEVICE = DISPLAY command in CONFIG.SYS; then restart DOS.

Codepage operation not supported on this device

The device may be one that does not support code pages, or its name may have been improperly entered or not defined. Verify the spelling of the device on the command line and make sure that it is not a file name. Check the CONFIG.SYS file to make sure it contains the device name. If it does not, add the device name to the DEVICE = command and restart DOS. Then reissue the MODE command.

Codepages cannot be prepared

Either code pages are duplicated on the device or there are more code pages specified than are allowable. Check the number of allowable code pages by using the MODE/STATUS command; then respecify the MODE command.

Current keyboard does not support this codepage

Alter the KEYB specification for the required code page and reissue the MODE PREPARE command for that code page.

Device error during Status
Device error during Prepare
Device error during Select
Device error during write of font file to device

The device may not support code page switching, or it may have been defined improperly. Check the CONFIG.SYS file to make sure the device is named; then restart DOS, and reissue the MODE command.

Device or codepage missing from font file

During a PREPARE operation, DOS could not find a definition of the indicated code page for the device. Reissue the MODE command, using a code page that the device supports (check the printer documentation). If this error occurs, you will need to prepare all code pages again by using MODE PREPARE.

Device *ddd* not prepared

A device must be prepared by using the MODE PREPARE command before a MODE SELECT operation can be performed. Use the MODE PREPARE command to pass code page definitions to the specified device.

Error during read of font file

There is an unrecoverable I/O error in that file. Restore the file from a master copy, or direct MODE to an alternate device and reissue the command to see if that device can access the file.

Failure to access Codepage Font File

Verify the spelling of the file name and make sure it is available; then reissue the MODE command.

Font file contents invalid

The font file is not in the proper format. Make sure that you have entered the file name correctly. If so, copy the file again from a master copy. If this error occurs, you will need to prepare all code pages again by using MODE PREPARE.

Illegal device name

The specified printer must be LPT1, LPT2, or LPT3; the asynchronous adapter must be COM1, COM2, COM3, or COM4.

Infinite retry not supported on network printer

Printer errors cannot be detected through a network interface; do not use the P option with a network printer.

Invalid baud rate specified

The baud rate must be either 110, 150, 300, 600, 1200, 2400, 4800, 9600, or 19200. You need to enter only the first two digits of the number.

Missing from the file is either the device ID or the codepage

Enter the correct code page or prepare the code pages again.

No codepage has been SELECTED

Use MODE to select a code page from the list of code pages that have been prepared.

Previously prepared codepage replaced

Use MODE/STATUS to check the list of code pages that have been defined to make sure that it is correct. The replacement may have been intentional. If not, use MODE PREPARE to correct the list.

Printer error

MODE could not set the printer mode either because an I/O error occurred or because the printer is out of paper, is not ready, or is off-line. Check the printer and try again.

NOTES

The different character sets available for version 3.3 of PC-DOS are code pages 437 (U.S., the default), 850 (multilingual), 860 (Portuguese), 863 (Canadian French), and 865 (Norwegian and Danish). In order to use a code page, it must be prepared for a specific device. Buffers should have been previously created for prepared code pages with

DEVICE = DISPLAY.SYS

and

DEVICE = PRINTER.SYS

if applicable. Several code pages can be prepared at once by using a code page list (*cplist*). For example,

**MODE LPT1: CP PREPARE = ((850,860,863)
5202.CPI)**

specifies the multilingual, Portuguese, and Canadian French character sets (code pages 850, 860, and 863) for the printer attached to LPT1 and specifes the character shapes for the IBM Quietwriter III printer. After a code page and device have been prepared, the code page may be activated by using the MODE SELECT command. The command

MODE LPT1: CP SELECT = 860

activates code page 860 (Portuguese) from the list of prepared code pages.

To determine the currently active code page, use the command

MODE LPT1: CP/STATUS

This command also returns a list of devices and code pages that have been prepared.

In addition, a code page may sometimes need to be reestablished (refreshed) if the printer has been turned off and then turned back on again. For further information about code pages and their uses, see the technical notes in the DOS documentation. Code pages are also discussed in the CHCP, KEYB, and NLSFUNC commands, and in Appendix B: The CONFIG.SYS file.

You can also use the following abbreviations:

- CP for CODEPAGE
- PREP for PREPARE
- SEL for SELECT
- REF for REFRESH
- STA for STATUS

MORE

Displaying One Screen of Data at a Time

Displays data one screen at a time.

VERSION

PC-DOS 2.0+
MS-DOS equivalent: **MORE** (2.0+)

TYPE

External

SYNTAX

[*d:*][*path*]   **MORE**

OPTIONS

d:path   Specifies the drive letter and path that contain
                the MORE command file.

MORE is used to display data one screen at a time to give you a
chance to review the contents of each screen before proceeding.

EXAMPLES

DIR ¦ MORE

displays the output from the DIR command one screen at a time.

MORE <OCT.RPT

displays the file OCT.RPT one screen at a time. (The less-than sign
tells DOS you are using input redirection.)

UNDO

Press Ctrl-C to cancel the MORE command.

NOTES

After MORE displays 23 lines (if you have a 25-line screen), it displays

– MORE –

and waits for you to press any key before it displays the next screen. If you do not use the < before a file name, MORE echoes each line you type.

NLSFUNC
Selecting Code Pages with CHCP

Allows you to select code pages (character sets) with the CHCP (change code page) command.

VERSION

PC-DOS 3.3

TYPE

External

SYNTAX

[*d:*][*path*]   **NLSFUNC**   [*fd:*][*fpath*][**COUNTRY.SYS**]

OPTIONS

d:path   Specifies the drive letter and path that contain the NLSFUNC command file.

fd:fpath
COUN-   Specifies the drive letter and path of the
TRY.SYS   COUNTRY.SYS file. Use only if this file is not located in the current directory.

NLSFUNC allows you to use the CHCP command to select additional character sets (code pages).

EXAMPLES

NLSFUNC

loads the NLSFUNC command, using the COUNTRY = command as defined in the CONFIG.SYS file.

NLSFUNC   C:\SPEC\COUNTRY.SYS

loads the NLSFUNC command while specifying that the COUN-
TRY.SYS file is stored in a directory named SPEC on drive C.

NOTES

NLSFUNC must be loaded before you use the CHCP command to
change code pages.

SEE ALSO

CHCP

PATH

Searching a Specified Path

Instructs DOS to search a specified path for programs not in the current directory.

VERSION

PC-DOS 2.0 +
MS-DOS equivalent: **PATH** (2.0 +)

TYPE

Internal

SYNTAX

PATH [[*d:*]*path*[;[*d:*]*path*]]

OPTIONS

d:	Specifies the letter of the drive(s) to be included in the search path.
path	Specifies the directory of path name(s) to be included in the search path.
;	Separates different drive letters and path names to be included in the PATH command statement.

PATH allows you to quickly access programs and batch files that may be stored in other subdirectories, no matter what directory you are in.

EXAMPLES

PATH   C:\BUSINESS\REPORTS;\BUSINESS\INVOICES

instructs DOS to look first in the default subdirectory, then in
C:\BUSINESS\REPORTS, and then in C:\BUSINESS\IN-
VOICES to find programs or files.

PATH

displays the current subdirectory on the default drive.

B>PATH   A:\BUSINESS;A:

instructs DOS to look first in the current subdirectory in drive B and
then in A:\BUSINESS and A:\.

MESSAGE

No path

No path has been defined for DOS to search. Use the PATH command to specify a path.

UNDO

To reset the search path to no extended search path, enter

PATH;

Designating a new PATH command supersedes an earlier PATH
command.

NOTES

You must specify each path completely. To have DOS search on
another drive, specify the drive designation.

SEE ALSO

SET

PRINT
Printing Files

Allows you to set up a print queue for printing files while continuing
to work in DOS.

VERSION

PC-DOS 2.0+
MS-DOS equivalent: **PRINT** (2.0+)

TYPE

External

SYNTAX

[*d:*][*path*] **PRINT** [*/D:device*][*/B:buffsiz*]
[*/U:busytick*][*/M:maxtick*][*/S:timeslice*][*/Q:quesiz*]
[*/C*][*/P*][*/T*] [*pd:*][*ppath*]*pfilename*(...)

OPTIONS

d:path	Specifies the drive letter and path of the PRINT command file.
/D:*device*	Specifies the print device. If not used, PRN is assumed. The /D parameter can only be specified the first time the PRINT command is invoked.
/B:*buffsiz*	Specifies the size in bytes of the internal buffer. The default is 512 bytes. The /B parameter can only be specified the first time the PRINT command is invoked.

/U:*busytick*   Specifies the number of clock ticks until the print device is available. The default value is 1. The /U parameter can only be specified the first time the PRINT command is invoked.

/M:*maxtick*   Specifies the number of clock ticks for which the print device is available to the PRINT command. The default is 2, and the value can be between 1 and 255. You need only specify the /M parameter the first time the PRINT command is invoked.

/S:*timeslice*   Specifies the time slice value. The default is 8 time slices, and the value can be between 1 and 255. The /S parameter can only be specified the first time the PRINT command is invoked.

/Q:*quesiz*   Specifies the number of files you can place in the print queue. The default is 10, and the value can be between 1 and 32 files. The /Q parameter can only be specified the first time the PRINT command is invoked.

/C   Specifies which file or files are to be removed from the print queue (canceled). The preceding file name and all subsequent file names on the command line are canceled until a /P parameter is encountered on the command line.

/P   Specifies that the preceding file name as well as any file names following the /P are to be added to the print queue, until another /C occurs in the command line.

/T   Removes all files from the print queue. Cancels printing of the file currently printed, displays cancellation message, and advances paper to the next page.

pd:ppath   Specifies the file(s) to be printed.
pfilename(...)

PRINT   BUSINESS.RPT

prints the file BUSINESS.RPT.

PRINT   BUSINESS.RPT   *.BAS

prints the file BUSINESS.RPT as well as all files with the extension
.BAS in the current directory.

Cannot use PRINT - use NET PRINT

PRINT cannot be used with a network fileserver; use NET PRINT
instead.

**Errors on list device indicate that
it may be off-line. Please check**

This message appears only when a new PRINT command is entered
while the device is off-line.

File not in print queue

The file you specified to cancel is not in the queue.

List output is not assigned to a device

The device is not valid; enter the PRINT command again, this time
using a valid device name.

xxxx* error on file *yyyy

While trying to read data from file *yyyy*, a disk error (type *xxxx*)
occurred. Check to make sure that the disk drive is ready and issue
the PRINT command again.

| UNDO |

To cancel all files in the print queue, enter

PRINT   /T

To remove specific files from the print queue, use the /C parameter. For example, the command

PRINT   /C   ACCTS.*

removes all files named ACCTS, regardless of extension, in the current directory from the print queue.

| NOTES |

The first time you use the command, you will be asked to specify the name of the device; do not use a colon at the end of the device name. When you add files to the queue, they must be in the current directory. However, you can change to another directory and then add files to the queue. The PRINT command increases the resident size of DOS by approximately 3600 bytes.

PROMPT

Changing the System Prompt

Allows you to change the DOS prompt.

VERSION

PC-DOS 2.0 +
MS-DOS equivalent: **PROMPT** (2.0 +)

TYPE

Internal

SYNTAX

PROMPT [*prompt*]

OPTIONS

The *prompt* can be any literal message displayed on the screen, and it can include any of the following special characters:

$t	Current time
$d	Current date
$n	Default drive
$p	Current path
$v	DOS version number
$g	Greater-than character (>)
$l	Less-than character (<)
$b	Vertical bar (|)

$q	Equal sign (=)
$_	Starts a new line (enters carriage-return/line-feed sequence)
$h	Backspaces and erases last character
$e	ESCAPE character (ASCII 27)

EXAMPLES

PROMPT $t $b $d $b ng
BEFORE: A>
AFTER: 12:09:33.55 | Thu 9-10-87 | A>

PROMPT   Command:
BEFORE: C>
AFTER: Command:

PROMPT   Good morning$_Today is $d
BEFORE: C>
AFTER: Good morning
             Today is Thu 9-10-87

PROMPT can also be used to display the current path at the prompt before the greater-than sign by entering the command as

PROMPT pg
BEFORE: C>
AFTER: C:\WP\LETTER>

UNDO

Enter

PROMPT

(with no prompt string) to reset the DOS prompt to the default prompt.

NOTES

All changes to the DOS prompt made with the PROMPT command remain in effect until you reboot the computer or enter a new PROMPT command. To maintain a consistent DOS prompt different from the default prompt, enter the appropriate PROMPT command in your AUTOEXEC.BAT file.

SEE ALSO

SET
Appendix A: Batch Files

RECOVER
Recovering Damaged Files

Recovers damaged files.

VERSION

PC-DOS 2.0+
MS-DOS equivalent: **RECOVER** (2.0+)

TYPE

External

SYNTAX

[*d:*][*path*]   **RECOVER**   [*rd:*][*rpath*]*rfilename*

or

[*d:*][*path*]   **RECOVER**   *rd:*

OPTIONS

d:path	Specifies the drive letter and directory path that contain the RECOVER command file.
rd:rpath rfilename	Specifies the file to be recovered.

RECOVER is used when you receive a "bad sector" error message to recover a damaged file. In using this command, you recover the data in a file with the bad sector minus the data in the bad sector.

EXAMPLES

RECOVER   B:REPORT2

recovers the file in drive B named REPORT2.

RECOVER   A:

recovers all of the files on the disk in drive A.

MESSAGES

Cannot RECOVER to a network drive

You cannot use the RECOVER command on a network drive. Pause the fileserver and then issue a RECOVER command again.

Warning - directory full
***xxx* file(s) recovered**

There is not enough space in the directory. Copy some of its files onto another disk and then reissue the RECOVER command.

NOTES

When you use RECOVER, it creates a new file with the same name that contains all the data in the original file except the data that was located in bad sectors. Also, RECOVER will not recover files that have been erased. If you use RECOVER on a disk that has a bad sector in its directory, each file name will have the form FILE*nnn*.REC, with the number *nnn* indicating the order in which the files were recovered. You will have to rename each file on the recovered disk by determining the contents of each file and naming it again. Wildcards may be used, but only the first matching file name will be used. Once you have used RECOVER, there is no way to reverse the recovery process.

SEE ALSO

CHKDSK

RENAME (REN)
Renaming Files

Changes the name of a file.

VERSION

PC-DOS: all
MS-DOS equivalent: **RENAME (REN)** (all)

TYPE

Internal

SYNTAX

REN   [*d:*][*path*]*filename*   *nfilename*

OPTIONS

d:path filename	Specifies the drive, path, and file name of the file to be renamed.
nfilename	Specifies the new name to be assigned to the file (must be on the same drive and path as the file to be renamed).

EXAMPLES

REN   **TEST**   **TEST1**
BEFORE: TEST
AFTER: TEST1

```
REN  *.CAP  *.SET
```
BEFORE: LETTER.CAP
ACCT.CAP
.
.
.
AFTER: LETTER.SET
ACCT.SET
.
.
.

UNDO

Repeat the REN command to rename the newly named file to its original file name.

MESSAGES

Duplicate file name or file not found

The file already exists on the drive/directory specified with the name you are trying to assign, or the file to be renamed cannot be found. Check to see that you have entered the file name correctly; then reissue the REN command.

Missing filename

The file name for the required *nfilename* parameter was not included.

NOTES

The old name must occur first and the new name must occur second. REN will not allow two files to have the same name at the same time, so you must use an intermediate name to switch the names of two files. Never rename special files that application programs require to operate.

SEE ALSO

COPY

REPLACE

Replacing Selected Files

Allows you to copy or add files selectively to target drives and directories.

VERSION

PC-DOS 3.2+
MS-DOS equivalent: **REPLACE** (3.2+)

TYPE

External

SYNTAX

[*d:*][*path*]   **REPLACE**   [*sd:*][*spath*]*sfilename*
[*td:*][*tpath*]   [/A][/P][/D][/R][/S][/W]

OPTIONS

d:path	Specifies the drive letter and directory that contain the REPLACE command file.
sd:spath *sfilename*	Specifies the source file(s) to be copied.
td:tpath	Specifies the target drive and directory.
/A	Copies all files from the source that do not exist on the target.
/P	Prompts for each file replacement.
/D	Copies only those files newer than the files on the target.

/R	Replaces read-only files on the target.
/S	Searches all the directories on the target for files that match the source file name.
/W	Prompts for insertion of a target disk before replacing begins.

REPLACE allows you to copy from a source disk those files that do not already exist on the target disk or that exist on both disks but are in an updated version on the source disk.

EXAMPLES

REPLACE   B:*.*   C:\REPORTS/A

copies all files in the root directory on drive B that are not already in the REPORTS directory of drive C.

REPLACE   A:*.TXT   C:\TEXT/A/P

adds all files with a .TXT extension on drive A to the TEXT directory on drive C if they are not there already. You will be prompted to confirm each file to be copied.

REPLACE   A:*.TXT   C:\TEXT/D

copies only those files with a .TXT extension on drive A that are newer than the files in the TEXT directory on drive C.

MESSAGES

Add d:\path\filename?

Enter Y to add the file to the target.

No files added

All the files on the source already exist on the target. No further action is required.

No files found

No files described in the argument were found on the source. No further action is required.

NOTES

The /A and /S options cannot be used together.

SEE ALSO

COPY

RESTORE

Restoring Backed-up Files

Restores backed-up files.

PC-DOS 2.0 + (revised in PC-DOS 3.3)
MS-DOS equivalent: **RESTORE** (2.0 +)

External

[*d:*][*path*] **RESTORE** *sd:* [*td:*][*tpath*]*tfilename*
[**/S**][**/P**][**/B**:*mm-dd-yy*] [**/A**:*mm-dd-yy*][**/M**][**/N**]
[**/L**:*time*][**/E**:*time*]

d:path	Specifies the drive letter and directory path that contain the RESTORE command.
sd:	Specifies the drive that contains the files to be backed up (source).
td:tpath *tfilename*	Specifies where you want backed up files to be restored to and which files from the source you want copied.
/S	Restores files in subdirectories of the directory you specify as well as in that directory.

/P   Prompts you for whether to restore files that
                have been altered since the last backup and
                those marked read-only.

/B:*mm-dd-yy*   Restores files modified on or before the date
                specified (PC-DOS 3.3).

/A:*mm-dd-yy*   Restores files modified on or after the date
                specified (PC-DOS 3.3).

/M   Restores files that have been modified or del-
                eted since they were backed up (PC-DOS 3.3).

/N   Restores files that are no longer on the target
                disk (PC-DOS 3.3).

/L:*time*   Restores only those files that were modified at
                or later than the specified time (PC-DOS 3.3).

/E:*time*   Restores only those files that were modified at or
                earlier than the specified time (PC-DOS 3.3).

RESTORE is used to copy disk files that were backed up with the
BACKUP command back onto the hard disk.

EXAMPLES

RESTORE B: C: /S

restores to drive C all files on drive B, including any files that were
backed up from subdirectories of the current directory on drive C.

RESTORE B: C:\report?.* /P

restores to drive C all files that have a file name of REPORT plus
any character, prompting you for read-only files and files changed
since the last backup.

RESTORE B: C:\GAMES

restores to drive C all files in the GAMES directory.

MESSAGES

Backup file sequence error

Parts of the file that is to be restored are on more than one disk. You inserted a disk that does not have the beginning portion of the file. Run RESTORE again, starting with the correct file.

Not able to restore file * * *

A file-sharing conflict exists, and the file you want to restore cannot be opened.

Restore file sequence error

You did not insert the disks in sequence. Reissue the RESTORE command, this time inserting the disks in order.

Source does not contain backup files

The source does not contain the backup files you specified. Locate the correct backup files and try again.

Source path required

Specify a source path and try again.

System files restored
The target disk may not be bootable

If the system files from a previous version of DOS were restored instead of those for the current version of DOS you are using, the resulting disk may not boot the system. Use the SYS command to transfer the current system files to the disk; then copy COM-MAND.COM onto the disk.

Target is full

Delete any unnecessary files and try again, or use a disk that is empty.

The last file was not restored

Either there was not enough room on the disk to restore the last file, or you stopped the RESTORE operation. Delete files on the disk to make space and reissue the RESTORE command. If you stopped the RESTORE operation, you may reissue the RESTORE command, continuing with the file where you left off.

Warning! Diskette is out of sequence
Replace the diskette or continue
Strike any key when ready

If you are sure that no files on the skipped disk would be restored, you may press any key to continue. Otherwise, replace the skipped disk.

Warning! File *xx*
is a read only file
Replace the file (Y/N)?

Enter Y to replace the file or N if you do not want to replace it.

Warning! File *xx*
was changed after it was backed up
Replace the file (Y/N)?

Enter Y to replace the file or N if you do not want to replace it.

Warning! No files were found to restore

No backup files were found matching your specification. Check the specification and try again.

Warning! Target is full

No more files can be restored to that target device without deleting some of its files first.

NOTES

Wildcards are permitted. If you specify a path without a file name, all files in that directory are restored. If you have backed up files to more than one disk, RESTORE will prompt you to insert them. Insert them in the order in which BACKUP created them.

RESTORE does not restore system files to create a bootable disk. Do not use RESTORE if JOIN, ASSIGN, or SUBST were in effect during the backup or if APPEND is in effect.

SEE ALSO

APPEND
ASSIGN
BACKUP
JOIN
SUBST
SYS

RMDIR (RD)

Removing Directories

Deletes a directory.

VERSION

PC-DOS 2.0 +
MS-DOS equivalent: **RMDIR (RD)** (2.0 +)

TYPE

Internal

SYNTAX

RMDIR   [*d:*]*path*

or

RD   [*d:*]*path*

OPTIONS

> *d:path*   Specifies the drive and path of the directory to
>   be removed.

RD is used to remove a subdirectory that is no longer required.

EXAMPLE

RD   C:\WP\FILES\LETTERS

deletes the subdirectory LETTERS.

MESSAGE

Invalid path, not directory, or directory not empty

Either one of the names you specified was not a directory or was the current directory (which you cannot remove), or the directory you are trying to remove still contains files (other than the . and .. files) and/or subdirectories. Either check the directory name, change to a different directory, or delete the contents of the directory and then reissue the RMDIR command.

UNDO

Use the MKDIR command to recreate a subdirectory that you removed in error.

NOTES

Only empty subdirectories may be removed. A subdirectory is empty when . and .. are the only entries in it. Remove all files from a subdirectory by using the DEL or ERASE command first. Only the last subdirectory in the path you specify will be removed. You cannot remove the subdirectory you are currently in; you must change to another directory first. In addition, you cannot delete the root directory.

SEE ALSO

CD
DEL/ERASE

SELECT

Selecting Format When Installing DOS

Installs DOS on a new disk with the keyboard layout, date, and time format of your choice.

VERSION

PC-DOS 3.0 +
MS-DOS equivalent: **SELECT** (3.0 +)

TYPE

External

SYNTAX

[*d:*][*path*] **SELECT** [*sd:*] [*td:*][*tpath*] *xxx* *yy*

OPTIONS

d:path	Specifies the drive letter and path that contain the SELECT command file.
sd:	Designates the source drive (only A: or B: are valid drive letters). If this parameter is omitted, A: is used. If you specify a source drive, you must specify a target drive (see below).
td:tpath	Specifies the target drive letter and the path where the DOS commands are to be copied to. If the drive parameter is omitted, B: is used. If the path parameter is omitted, the files are copied to the root directory on the target.

xxx	Specifies the country code that instructs DOS to use the date, time, collating sequence, capitalization, and folding format for that country.
yy	Specifies the abbreviation for the keyboard code for the country. When specifying the country and keyboard codes, you can select from the following:

Country	Country Code	Keyboard Code
United States	001	US
France	033	FR
Spain	034	SP
Italy	039	IT
United Kingdom	044	UK
Germany	049	GR

EXAMPLE

SELECT 033 FR

copies DOS from a disk in drive A to a disk in drive B and configures the keyboard with the French layout. Dates, times, capitalization, and collating sequence will be formatted according to the custom of that country.

MESSAGES

Failure to access COUNTRY.SYS

Make sure that the source disk contains the COUNTRY.SYS file; then repeat the SELECT command.

Failure to access KEYBOARD.SYS

Make sure that the source disk contains the KEYBOARD.SYS file; then repeat the SELECT command.

Invalid keyboard code

Check the two-digit keyboard code and try again.

Invalid signature in COUNTRY.SYS file

The header for the COUNTRY.SYS file has been altered. Use the original DOS start-up disk with the master COUNTRY.SYS file on it and repeat the command.

Invalid signature in KEYBOARD.SYS file

The header for the KEYBOARD.SYS file has been altered. Use the original DOS start-up disk with the master COUNTRY.SYS file on it and repeat the command.

Read error, COUNTRY.SYS

An I/O error has occurred. You may be using a damaged disk. Insert the master DOS start-up disk and try again.

Read error, KEYBOARD.SYS

An I/O error has occurred. You may be using a damaged disk. Insert the master DOS start-up disk and try again.

SELECT is used to install DOS the first time. SELECT erases everything on the specified target and then installs DOS. Do you want to continue (Y/N)?

Type Y to have DOS execute the SELECT command that you have entered. Type N to abort the SELECT command.

NOTES

Because SELECT uses the FORMAT command, all data on the target disk will be destroyed. When using this command, the target drive must be different from the source drive.

The default values are for the United States: they are mm-dd-yy and hh:mm:ss:dd for the date and time. The decimal indicator is the period (.), and the currency symbol is the dollar sign ($).

SET
Setting Operating Parameters

Inserts specified names (strings) into the command processor's environment.

VERSION

PC-DOS 2.0 +
MS-DOS equivalent: **SET** (2.0 +)

TYPE

Internal

SYNTAX

SET   [*name* = [*parameter*]]

OPTIONS

name   Specifies a variable.

parameter   Specifies a new value for the environment.

SET is used to pass arguments to application programs or to batch files that look into the DOS environment for operating parameters.

EXAMPLES

SET   FIL = \PROGFIL

instructs DOS to look in the \PROGFIL directory when an application program interrogates the environment for FIL.

SET

displays the names that have been set in the environment, such as the path and the prompt.

SET   NAME = HAROLD

allows you to call the value assigned to NAME from a batch file. In the batch file, you must enclose the variable NAME in percent signs, which indicate to DOS that a variable is being used rather than a command-line argument (see Appendix A for more information about batch files and using variables in them). To call the value assigned to NAME—for example, to change to Harold's directory—you would enter the line in the batch file as

CD \%NAME%

If ECHO were on, you would see

CD \HAROLD

when this line was executed.

UNDO

To remove a string from the environment, you merely repeat the SET command using the *name* parameter without specifying any other parameter. For example, to remove NAME = HAROLD from the environment, simply enter

SET   NAME =

NOTES

All names are converted to uppercase in the environment, but parameters will remain uppercase and lowercase as you enter them. The SET command is useful for allowing application programs or batch files to be written generically while you assign values dynamically in the course of a program or batch file.

One of the strings placed in the environment automatically is the COMSPEC= parameter, which describes the path that DOS uses to reload the command processor when required. To use a command processor other than COMMAND.COM, you need to use the COMSPEC= parameter in the SET command. Always use the drive letter in the path used to describe the location of COMMAND.COM or your own command processor.

SEE ALSO

Appendix A: Batch Files

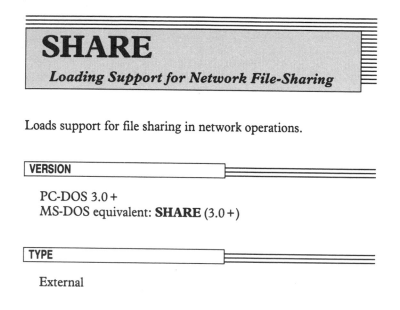

SHARE

Loading Support for Network File-Sharing

Loads support for file sharing in network operations.

VERSION

PC-DOS 3.0 +
MS-DOS equivalent: **SHARE** (3.0 +)

TYPE

External

SYNTAX

[*d:*][*path*]   **SHARE**   [**/F:***filespace*][**/L:***locks*]

OPTIONS

d:path	Specifies the drive letter and path that contain the SHARE command file.
/F:*filespace*	Allocates file space in bytes for the area used to record information required for file-sharing. Each open file requires the length of the entire file name plus 11 bytes (default: 2038 bytes).
/L:*locks*	Allocates space for the number of locks used (default: 20 locks).

SHARE is required in network operations for sharing files.

SHARE   /F:3000/L:30

allocates 3000 bytes to the file-sharing buffer size and allows for 30 locks.

Incorrect parameter

Check the command syntax and retry.

Not enough memory

Insufficient memory is available to run SHARE.

The SHARE command needs to be called only once each time you boot and are using a network.

SORT
Sorting Text Data

Instructs DOS to sort text data.

VERSION

PC-DOS 2.0+
MS-DOS equivalent: **SORT** (2.0+)

TYPE

External

SYNTAX

[*d:*][*path*] **SORT** [/R][/ + *n*]

OPTIONS

d:path	Specifies the drive letter and path that contain the SORT command file.
/R	Sorts in reverse ASCII order.
/ + *n*	Sorts lines by their *n*th column instead of by the character in the first column of each line. The *n* is an integer value.

EXAMPLES

SORT <**TEST.TXT**

Assuming TEST.TXT consists of a list of names, this command sorts the file alphabetically and displays the results on the screen.

The less-than sign instructs SORT to take its input from the file instead of from the keyboard.

SORT   / + 20   <TEST.TXT

Assuming TEST.TXT consists of a list of names as well as phone numbers that begin on column 20, this command sorts the list by phone number order.

DIR ¦SORT>PRN:

prints a directory listing in alphabetical order.

NOTES

You can redirect the output of the SORT command from standard output (the screen) by using redirection or piping. Likewise, you can instruct SORT to take its input from other than the standard input (the keyboard). The maximum size of a file to be sorted is 63K.

The SORT command sorts characters according to their binary values, except that lowercase letters are equal to uppercase letters (A = a) and characters above 127 are collated according to the rules of the currently selected country code.

SEE ALSO

FIND
MORE

SUBST

Substituting Drive Designators

Allows you to substitute a different drive designator for a drive or a path.

VERSION

PC-DOS 3.0 +
MS-DOS equivalent: **SUBST** (3.0 +)

TYPE

External

SYNTAX

[*d:*][*path*]   **SUBST**   *d1:*   *d2:path*

or

[*d:*][*path*]   **SUBST**   *d1:* /**D**

or

[*d:*][*path*]   **SUBST**

OPTIONS

d:path	Specifies the drive letter and path that contain the SUBST command file.
d1:	Indicates the new drive designator.
d2:path	Indicates the existing drive and path.
/D	Deletes the specified substitution.

EXAMPLES

SUBST   D: C:\VERY\LONG\PATH\NAME

Whenever D: is used, DOS substitutes the path name C:\VERY\LONG\PATH\NAME.

SUBST

displays the currently defined substitutions.

MESSAGE

Cannot SUBST to a network drive

You cannot substitute a drive for a network path or substitute a network drive for a local path.

UNDO

To discontinue the currently defined substitutions, enter

SUBST   /D

for each substitution.

NOTES

Because SUBST substitutes drive letters for path names, it can be used to fool programs that do not recognize path names into using them indirectly. SUBST can be used with certain programs that do not recognize paths and can also be used as a type of shorthand for long path names.

SYS

Copying System Files to Another Disk

Copies the DOS files onto another disk.

VERSION

PC-DOS 1.0+
MS-DOS equivalent: **SYS** (2.0+; **SYSCOPY** in earlier versions)

TYPE

External

SYNTAX

[*d:*][*path*]   **SYS**   *cd:*

OPTIONS

d:path   Specifies the drive letter and path that contain
the SYS command file.

cd: Specifies the letter of the disk drive that
contains the disk you want the SYS files
copied to.

EXAMPLES

SYS   B:

copies the DOS files to the disk in drive B.

```
SYS  B:
COPY  COMMAND.COM  B:
```

copies the DOS files to the disk in drive B and makes the disk bootable by copying the COMMAND.COM file.

MESSAGES

Cannot SYS to a network drive

You cannot use SYS on a network. Pause the fileserver and then issue the SYS command.

No room for system on destination disk

There is not enough space for the system files on the destination disk. Format a new disk with FORMAT/S and then reissue the command.

No system on default drive

DOS cannot locate the system files to be transferred. Select a disk that has the DOS files on it and try again.

NOTES

The target disk must either have an empty root directory, have been formatted with the /S option of the FORMAT command, or have been formatted with the /B option of the FORMAT command. If you use the SYS command on a disk that has not been properly formatted, you may lose data from it. The SYS command does not copy the COMMAND.COM file, which is required to make a disk bootable.

SEE ALSO

FORMAT

TIME

Entering the Current Time

Displays the current time and allows you to reset the time.

VERSION

PC-DOS 2.0 + (revised from 1.0; revised again in 3.3)
MS-DOS equivalent: **TIME** (2.0 +; revised from 1.0)

TYPE

Internal

SYNTAX

TIME [*hh:mm*[:*ss*[.*xx*]]]

OPTIONS

hh	Hours
mm	Minutes
ss	Seconds
.xx	Hundredths of seconds

EXAMPLES

TIME   21:30

sets the time to 21:30:00:00 (9:30 p.m.).

TIME

returns the current time as indicated by the system clock and prompts you for a new time. You can accept the current time by pressing Return.

| MESSAGE |

Invalid time

Reenter the time in the correct format, with a colon (:) between hours and minutes as well as between minutes and seconds. Use a period (.) between seconds and hundredths of a second.

| UNDO |

If you set the time incorrectly, use the TIME command a second time and enter the current time.

| NOTES |

In version 3.3 of PC-DOS, the TIME command also changes the permanent clock, if the system has one.

| SEE ALSO |

DATE

TREE
Displaying Directory Trees

Displays all the directory paths on a specified drive.

VERSION

PC-DOS 2.0 +
MS-DOS equivalent: **TREE** (2.0 +)

TYPE

External

SYNTAX

[*d:*][*path*]   **TREE**   [*pd:*][**/F**]

OPTIONS

d:path	Specifies the drive letter and path that contain the TREE command.
pd:	Specifies the drive whose directory paths you want to display. If omitted, the default drive is used.
/F	Displays all the file names within each subdirectory.

The TREE command is used to quickly view the structure of a hierarchically organized disk.

TREE C:

lists the directories on drive A, each with its full path name and its subdirectories shown in the following form:

DIRECTORY PATH LISTING FOR VOLUME 12
PATH: \REPORTS
SUB-DIRECTORIES: OCTOBER
                  NOVEMBER
PATH: \REPORTS\OCTOBER
SUB-DIRECTORIES: OCT5-10
                  OCT12-17
PATH: \REPORTS\NOVEMBER
SUB-DIRECTORIES: NOV9-14
                  NOV16-21

TREE C:/F

allows you to see the names of individual files in the subdirectories, and it returns (in part)

PATH: \REPORTS\NOVEMBER\NOV9-14
SUB-DIRECTORIES: NONE
FILES: NOV10.TXT
       NOV12.TXT
       NOV13.TXT

TYPE
Displaying the Contents of a File

Displays a file's contents on the screen.

VERSION

PC-DOS: all
MS-DOS equivalent: **TYPE** (all)

TYPE

Internal

SYNTAX

TYPE   [*d:*][*path*]*filename*

OPTIONS

d:path   Specifies the name and location of the file
filename   whose contents are to be displayed.

The TYPE command is used to view the contents of a file.

EXAMPLE

TYPE   NOVRPT.TXT
displays the contents of the file NOVRPT.TXT on the screen.

NOTES

The TYPE command continuously scrolls the file on the screen if it is longer than one screenful. To freeze the text on the screen, press Ctrl-Num Lock. To stop the TYPE command from presenting more of the file's contents on the screen, press Ctrl-C. Data will be unformatted except for standard paragraph indents and eight-character tabs. If you use the TYPE command to view binary files, program files, or files that contain control codes, their contents may be meaningless on the screen. A file that is in ASCII format is readable on the screen when the TYPE command is used.

SEE ALSO

PRINT

VER
Displaying the DOS Version

Displays the version of DOS you are using.

VERSION

PC-DOS 2.0+
MS-DOS equivalent: **VER** (2.0+)

TYPE

Internal

SYNTAX

VER

The VER command is used to determine which version of DOS a system is running under.

EXAMPLE

VER

returns

IBM Personal Computer DOS Version 3.30

if you are using PC-DOS 3.3.

VERIFY

Verifying Data

Verifies that data was correctly written on a disk.

VERSION

PC-DOS 2.0 +
MS-DOS equivalent: **VERIFY** (2.0 +)

TYPE

Internal

SYNTAX

VERIFY   [ON]

or

VERIFY   [OFF]

OPTIONS

ON   Turns verification on until the system is
            rebooted.

OFF   Turns verification off once it has been turned
            on.

The VERIFY command is used to confirm that information is
written correctly each time the system writes information.

EXAMPLE

VERIFY

displays whether VERIFY is currently turned on or off.

NOTES

With VERIFY on, DOS checks information each time it writes it to disk, which can slow writing speed slightly. You can also use the COPY command with the /V option if you prefer to verify on a case-by-case basis.

VOL

Displaying the Volume Name

Displays a disk's volume name.

VERSION

PC-DOS 2.0+
MS-DOS equivalent: **VOL** (2.0+)

TYPE

Internal

SYNTAX

VOL [*d:*]

OPTIONS

d:　　　　　Specifies the disk to check.

The VOL command is used to determine the volume label given
to a disk when it was formatted.

EXAMPLE

VOL

displays the volume label entered when the disk on the current drive
was formatted. If the volume label is SCRIPTS, the message

Volume in drive C is SCRIPTS

is returned.

XCOPY
Copying Selected Files

Allows you to selectively copy groups of files.

VERSION

PC-DOS 3.2 +
MS-DOS equivalent: **XCOPY** (3.2 +)

TYPE

External

SYNTAX

[*d:*][*path*] **XCOPY** [*sd:*][*spath*]*sfilename*
[*td:*][*tpath*][*tfilename*] [/A][/D][/E][/M][/P][/S][/V][/W]

OPTIONS

d:path	Specifies the drive letter and path that contain the XCOPY command file.
sd:spath *sfilename*	Specifies the drive, directory, or file from which you want XCOPY to copy (source).
td:tpath *tfilename*	Specifies the drive, directory, and file name to which you want the file(s) copied (target).
/A	Copies only those files whose archive bit is set to on.
/D	Copies only those files whose date is the same or later than the date specified in the form /D:mm-dd-yy, /D:dd-mm-yy, or /D:yy-mm-dd.

/E   Creates subdirectories on the target when used
            with the /S option even if the corresponding
            subdirectories in the source are empty;
            otherwise they are not created.

/M   Copies files whose archive bit is set to on and
            also clears the archive bit.

/P   Prompts before copying each file.

/S   Copies files in subdirectories as well as in the
            source directory; creates subdirectories if
            necessary.

/V   Instructs DOS to verify that all files have been
            written correctly.

/W   Prompts you to press any key before copying
            files, thus allowing you to insert a new disk.

The XCOPY command is used to copy files by specifying only a
directory or drive without indicating file names.

EXAMPLES

XCOPY   A:\   C:\

copies all files in the root directory of the disk in drive A to the root
directory of drive C.

XCOPY   B: /D:11-22-87

copies all files dated on or after November 22, 1987, from a disk in
drive B to the current directory.

XCOPY   C:\REPORTS   D:/S/E

copies all files in the REPORTS subdirectory on drive C as well as
all files in its subdirectories to drive D and creates equivalently
named subdirectories, even if they are empty.

XCOPY   C: A:/S/M

copies all files on drive C that have changed since the last backup
and clears the archive bit after the copy.

MESSAGES

Cannot perform a cyclic copy

You probably specified the /S option while the source was directly above the destination subdirectory, so the destination is considered to be part of the source. Use a temporary file or disk to contain the source directory at the same or a lower level than the destination directory.

Cannot XCOPY from a reserved device

You have specified a printer or an asynchronous port as the source. The source must be a file. Put the source data into a file and reissue the XCOPY command.

Does < path name > specify a file or directory name on the target (F = file, D = directory)?

XCOPY did not find a directory named < *path name* >. Enter D if you are copying a directory or F if you are copying only one file.

File cannot be copied onto itself

You tried to copy a file using the same name, directory, and disk as the original. Reissue the XCOPY command, using a different name, or direct the copy to a different disk.

Lock violation

The source file is locked. Try again after a short time.

Too many open files

You need to reconfigure the system. Increase the FILES = value in your CONFIG.SYS file if it is less than 20.

NOTES

XCOPY allows you to copy only files whose archive bit is on (indicating it has been backed up since its last change) when you have used the /A or /M option. XCOPY works only within a single directory

unless the /S option is specified. The /S option does create subdirectories, but it does not replicate empty subdirectories unless used
with the /E option.

SEE ALSO

COPY
Appendix B: The CONFIG.SYS File

APPENDIX

Batch Files

A batch file contains a series of commands that DOS executes sequentially whenever you enter the name of the batch file and press Enter at the DOS prompt. The batch file name must contain the extension .BAT to execute. However, when running a batch file, you do not enter the .BAT extension as part of the command file name.

The batch file is saved as a DOS text file (in ASCII format). It can contain DOS commands and/or special batch file commands that are used only in batch files.

Batch files are frequently used to automate the execution of a group of commands that you find yourself having to enter manually over and over. These can include typical start-up, maintenance, and backup procedures as well as such simple tasks as renaming specific DOS commands to make them easier to remember and access (such as FORMAT A: to PREPARE).

Each command statement in the batch file is listed by line in the file, and DOS executes each statement in the order in which it is entered in the batch file. DOS will terminate the batch file as soon as it has executed the last command statement in the file. To terminate a batch file at any time before this, issue the BREAK command (either by pressing Ctrl-C or Ctrl-Break). When you issue the BREAK command during the execution of a batch file, DOS displays the message

Terminate batch job (Y/N)?

To have DOS to ignore the current command statement and execute the next command statement, thereby continuing the running of the rest of the batch file, type N. To terminate the execution of the current and all remaining command statements (that is, abort the batch file), type Y. (Note that some versions of DOS require that you press Enter after typing Y or N. Also, some commands that can be entered in a batch file will not respond to the BREAK command.)

Creating Batch Files

You can create a batch file using the COPY command, EDLIN (the line editor supplied with DOS), or any other editor or word processor that can save its text in ASCII format. When creating or saving the batch file, be sure to append the extension .BAT to the file name you assign to it.

To create a batch file using the COPY command, use the paradigm

COPY   CON   *filename*.**BAT**

where

> *filename*   Specifies the name you wish to assign to the batch file.

After entering this, you simply type in each command statement in the order you wish it to be processed when the batch file is executed. After typing in each command statement, you terminate the line by pressing the Enter key.

Once you have entered all of the command statements you wish to have in your batch file, you save it on disk (in the current directory) by pressing Ctrl-Z (you can also accomplish this by pressing F6 on IBM PCs and most compatibles) and the Enter key.

The Automatic Execution Batch File

You can create a special batch file, named AUTOEXEC.BAT, which contains all of the DOS commands that you wish to have invoked every time you start your computer. The command statements in the AUTOEXEC.BAT file often include such DOS commands as DATE, TIME, PROMPT, PATH, and SET. These can also include commands that execute special RAM-resident programs such as Lightning or SideKick or a menu program of your own design. Such a program would allow you to start up specific application programs available on your PC—dBASE III PLUS, Lotus 1-2-3, or WordPerfect, for example.

Every time you start your computer, DOS checks for the presence of the AUTOEXEC.BAT file on either the disk in drive A if you are using a two-floppy disk system, or in the root directory of drive C if you are using a hard disk system. If DOS locates such a file, it automatically executes the statements it contains upon completion of the boot sequence.

When you create the AUTOEXEC.BAT file, remember to include the DATE and TIME commands along with the other commands you wish executed each time you start the computer. (If your computer is equipped with a clock/calendar card, enter the appropriate commands to have the date and time read.) If you do not add these commands, DOS will no longer prompt you for the current date and time as part of the start-up procedure and, as a result, the files you create with your application programs will not be stamped with the correct date and time.

Consider the following example created with the COPY command and containing a sampling of DOS commands typically used in the AUTOEXEC.BAT file:

```
COPY  CON  AUTOEXEC.BAT
DATE
TIME
```

```
PROMPT   $p$g
PATH = C:\;C:\DOS;C:\BATCH
<Ctrl-Z>
```

After creating this AUTOEXEC.BAT file, when you start your computer DOS will first prompt you to update the date and time. Once you have responded to these commands, DOS changes the prompt so that it always displays the current directory, and then sets the path so that it will check the root, \DOS, and \BAT directories for any command that you enter, regardless of which directory you are in at the time.

Displaying Text on the Screen

The batch files that you create can contain messages that are displayed to alert the user to the underlying purpose of the batch file or to prompt the user to take a particular step—such as changing data disks—during a pause in the execution of a command. You can also add messages that are displayed as part of the ECHO command, which controls whether the command statements entered in the batch file are displayed to the user as they are executed by DOS.

Using the REM Command

One way to have text displayed on the screen during the execution of a batch command is with the use of the REM (remark) command

   REM   *remark*

where

      remark   Specifies the comment to be added to a batch file.

DOS will not try to execute a REM command, although it will display REM and the text that follows it on the screen unless it has previously executed an ECHO OFF statement (see Using the ECHO Command, which follows).

You can use the REM command to add messages to the batch file that help make clear its function and procedure. If you wish to add a nonprinting comment whose purpose is to document the use of particular commands in your batch file but that is never to be displayed on the screen to the user, you simply preface the text of this type of comment with a colon, as in:

:Start backup

Comments prefaced with a colon will appear when you use the TYPE command to display the contents of the batch file on your screen, or when you use the COPY or PRINT command to obtain a printout.

Using the PAUSE Command

You can also have messages displayed on the screen during a pause in the execution of batch file commands. The syntax for the PAUSE command is

PAUSE   *[message]*

where

   [message]   Specifies the message you want to have displayed
                    on the screen when PAUSE is invoked.

When DOS encounters a PAUSE statement, it pauses the execution of the commands in the batch file and displays your message on the screen, followed by its own message

Strike a key when ready. . .

on the line below. If you enter the PAUSE command without any message text, you will see only this DOS message instructing you to strike a key to continue the execution of the batch file.

When you use the PAUSE command, the word *PAUSE* is always displayed on the screen along with the message you have entered (just as when using the REM command). If the batch file has executed an ECHO OFF command before it encounters your PAUSE command, neither the word *PAUSE* nor the text of your message will be displayed on the screen. Only the DOS message about striking a key to continue will be visible (see Using the ECHO Command, which follows).

Using the ECHO Command

When DOS executes the commands in a batch file, it can display each command statement on the screen as it is executed. You can enter the ECHO command in the batch file to control whether the command statements are displayed. The syntax is

ECHO   [OFF]

or

ECHO   [ON]

where

OFF   Suppresses the display of command state-
                ments during the execution.

ON   Used if you wish to have subsequent com-
                mands displayed on the screen during the exe-
                cution of the batch file.

Note that if you enter the ECHO command in a batch file (or at the DOS prompt) without using either the ON or OFF parameters, DOS responds by displaying the current state of the ECHO command. You will see either *ECHO is on* or *ECHO is off*.

If you are using DOS 3.3, you can also suppress the display of a command statement in the batch file by prefacing it with the @ symbol. For example, entering

@VERIFY   ON

will prevent the VERIFY ON command from being displayed. However, each command statement that you wish to suppress must be prefaced by an @ symbol. If you use @ECHO OFF, the ECHO OFF command as well as all subsequent statements are automatically suppressed until an ECHO ON command occurs.

When ECHO is off, only the display of the command statements in the batch file will be suppressed. DOS will continue to display any message that is normally shown after a particular command has been processed. For instance, if your batch file contains the statement

ECHO   OFF

followed by a command to copy a particular file from one directory to another, you will still see the DOS message

   1 File(s) copied

although you will not see the contents of the COPY command itself on the line above it. Note that you can often get rid of these messages by redirecting output to NUL:

   COPY *.* A: >NUL

You can use the ECHO command to display messages to the user. First, set ECHO to off. Then, enter an ECHO command followed by at least one space and the text of your message. When you use the ECHO command in this way, only your message is displayed on the screen. DOS does not include the command word (ECHO) as it does when displaying messages with the REM or PAUSE commands.

For example, you could have your batch file display a prompt to insert a data disk in drive A by using the ECHO and PAUSE commands as follows:

   ECHO   OFF
   .
   .
   .
   ECHO   Insert data disk in drive A
   PAUSE

When the batch file executes these last two commands, you see only

   Insert data disk in drive A
   Strike a key when ready. . .

on the screen. ECHO does not appear along with the prompt message, but the separate PAUSE command causes the *Strike a key when ready. . .* message to be displayed.

When you use the ECHO command to display messages and prompts, be sure that it is preceded by an ECHO OFF statement (or an @ symbol if you are using DOS 3.3) in the batch file. Otherwise, you will see the ECHO command statement containing the message as well as the message itself when the batch file is run.

Note that the use of the REM, PAUSE, and ECHO commands to display on-screen messages slows down the execution of the batch file appreciably. If you need to include extensive instructions for a particular batch file, use the TYPE command to have them displayed on the screen.

Replaceable Parameters

You can define parameters (or arguments) that are passed to particular command statements in a batch file with the use of replaceable or dummy parameters. This makes the batch file more flexible because you get to define the arguments to be passed to the command statements at the time you execute the batch file.

You can define up to ten different replaceable parameters to be used in a batch file. Each one is given a number between 0 and 9 preceded by the percent sign, as in %1, %2, and so on. Note, however, that the replaceable parameter %0 represents a special case: it is always replaced with the file name of the batch file.

The other nine replaceable parameters have no such fixed replacements: you can make then stand for DOS commands, file names, parts of file names (such as extensions), directory paths, and the like. For instance, you could use replaceable parameters to create a batch file named WHEREIS.BAT that locates a particular file for you. This batch file contains only a single command statement using the replaceable argument, as follows:

```
CHKDSK   /V ¦ FIND   "%1"
```

The CHKDSK command with the /V parameter lists all of the files and subdirectories for the current directory and pipes this information to the FIND command.

The FIND command contains the replaceable parameter %1. When you execute the WHEREIS.BAT file, you enter the file name you wish to locate along with the batch file name. To locate a file called LOAN.FRM on the hard disk, you run the batch file by entering

```
WHEREIS   LOAN.FRM
```

DOS will then execute WHEREIS.BAT as though you had entered

CHKDSK /V¦FIND "LOAN.FRM"

as the command statement. If this file is located in C:\WP-\FORMS, DOS will respond by displaying

C:\WP\FORMS\LOAN.FRM

As you can see, you can use this same batch file to search for any file or group of files, simply by entering a different file name at the time you execute it.

In complex batch files, you may find that ten replaceable parameters are not sufficient. In such a case, you can use the SHIFT command. SHIFT discards each argument after it has been acted upon, replacing it with the next argument so that after the first argument is processed, the second becomes the first, the third the second, and so on. After you use the SHIFT command, the 0% argument is never acted upon, since the %n argument becomes the %($n-1$) argument. Note that SHIFT is useful in loops, which are described later in this appendix.

Passing Arguments from the Environment

As noted in the SET reference entry, you can specify a set of strings that the batch files can refer to. For example, if you enter the SET command

SET REPORT = YREND

and have previously entered the following command line in a batch file

COPY %REPORT%.WK1 A:

the batch file will copy the file named YREND.WK1 to the floppy disk in drive A when the batch file is run.

Note that the replaceable argument in the batch file command line is enclosed in a pair of percent signs (%). This indicates to DOS that the argument is to be taken from the environment.

Loops in Batch Files

There are several methods for creating loops in batch files. If you want the entire batch file to repeat, you can use the %0 replaceable parameter as the last command. You will recall that %0 is always replaced with the file name of the batch file. When you add it as the last statement in a batch file, it causes all of the commands in the file to be repeated. For example, if you create a batch file named DIRA.BAT that contains the command statements

```
ECHO   OFF
ECHO   Insert new disk in drive A
PAUSE
DIR   A:/p
%0
```

the file will repeatedly prompt you to insert a different disk in drive A and then give you a directory listing of all of the files it contains when you press a key to continue. This batch file will continue to repeat until you press Ctrl-C or Ctrl-Break to terminate it.

The FOR Loop

To repeat a command within a batch file for a specific number of cases, you use the FOR command. The syntax for the FOR command is

FOR   %%_variable_ **IN   (**_set_**)   DO**   _command_

where

command   Specifies the command to be executed for each member listed in the (_set_) argument, in the order in which these members are entered. The _command_ argument can consist of only a single command, which can be another batch file command (except for the FOR command), an executable program, batch file, or DOS command. Note that you cannot nest FOR batch commands, which is why the _command_ argument cannot contain another FOR command statement.

set   Specifies files to be operated upon.

variable   Specifies the variable to be operated on by the *command*. Notice that a double percent sign is entered before the variable (usually, though not necessarily, a single letter) to distinguish it from a replaceable parameter.

Consider this example using the FOR command:

**FOR   %%A   IN   (1985.WK1   1986.WK1   1987.WK1)
   DO   COPY   %%A   %2**

In this batch file, the FOR command statement copies each of the three worksheet files listed in the (*set*) argument to the directory path entered when the batch file is run by passing it to the %2 replaceable parameter. Notice that the *command* argument in this example is actually COPY %%A, instead of just COPY.

The GOTO Command

You can also cause a batch file to execute (and sometimes repeat) a group of command statements in the file beginning at a specific point. To do this, you use the GOTO batch command. You indicate where in the batch file the commands are to be executed (or repeated) by using a label.

The syntax of the GOTO command is

GOTO   [:]/*label*

where

label   Specifies a character string of up to eight alphanumeric characters, and is not case-sensitive. By convention, alphabetic characters are entered in lowercase and the label name is prefaced by a colon. Note that the colon is mandatory before the actual label, but optional before the argument in the GOTO. The label, however, cannot contain a period (.).

When you use the GOTO command, DOS executes all of the command statements listed below the label until it reaches the end of the batch file or another GOTO statement telling it to begin reprocessing the commands or to process a new set of commands beneath another label.

Looping with the GOTO command can be illustrated by the following generalized form:

```
:label
command%1
.
.
.
command%n
SHIFT
GOTO   :label
```

Assuming that the commands listed below the :label contain replaceable parameters, with the use of the SHIFT batch command, this loop would be executed indefinitely (until you terminated the batch file by pressing Ctrl-C or Ctrl-Break).

Conditional Processing

The endless loop illustrated above is of limited use in batch files. It is much more common to use the GOTO command with conditional statements. That way, the commmands listed beneath the label are executed only when the condition is true. Using the GOTO command with conditions allows you to create batch files that branch according to the result of the condition.

In addition to using conditional processing to branch, you can also have command statements executed only when there is equivalency between two items or if a particular file exists.

The IF Command

The batch IF command is used to allow conditional execution of command statements. The syntax of the IF command is as follows:

```
IF  [NOT]  condition   command
```

If you wish to have branching occur as a result of the outcome of the condition, use this form:

IF *[NOT]* *condition* **GOTO** *[:]label*

There is no ELSE command in the batch file command vocabulary. If you wish to have the program branch to one set of commands if the condition is true and another if it is false, use this form:

IF *condition* **GOTO** *[:]labela*
GOTO *[:]labelb*

If the condition is true, execution jumps to the commands beneath label a. If it is false, it jumps to those beneath label b. Note that you do not have to use the second GOTO statement if the commands to be executed when the condition is false follow the IF statement directly.

Testing for Equivalence

The *condition* argument in an IF command can test for equivalence between two items. If they are found to be equivalent (that is, identical in terms of characters and case), then the command statement listed in the *command* argument is executed. When you test for equivalence, you use a double equal sign. The syntax is as follows:

IF *string1* = =*string2* *command*

Note that strings are case-sensitive.

For example, you could enter the following IF command:

IF **%1** = =**December** **GOTO** **:endofyr**

If you execute this batch file and enter December as the first replaceable parameter, the batch file will jump to the label :endofyr and execute the commands that are listed beneath it.

Testing for the Existence of a File

You test for the existence of a particular file as the *condition* argument of the IF command. The syntax for this use is as follows:

IF **EXIST** *[d:][path]filename* *command*

The options are as follows:

command   Specifies a command to be executed only when the file entered for the *d:path filename* argument is found on the drive/directory indicated (if these parameters are omitted, then in the current directory).

d:path   Specifies the file to be operated on.
filename

For example, you might have this IF command statement in a batch file:

IF   EXIST   4QTRTOTL   GOTO   :yrend

The commands beneath the :yrend label are executed only if DOS locates the file named 4QTRTOTL in the current directory. If this file is not found, this GOTO statement is ignored.

Chaining Batch Files

You can chain batch files by adding the name of the second batch file to be executed as the last statement in the command statements of the first batch file. Do not confuse chaining batch files with calling a new batch file as a subroutine. When chaining batch files, control does not return to the first batch file as when using subroutines (see the section on Using Subroutines, which follows). Because of this, reference to the second batch file must be entered as the last command statement in the first batch file. If it is not, the commands below this reference in the first file will never be executed.

Using Subroutines

To execute a second batch file as a subroutine (that is, have control returned to the first batch file upon execution of all command statements in the second file), you must load a second copy of the command processor, using the COMMAND command. The syntax is

COMMAND /C *batch*

where

/C   Tells DOS that this a secondary copy of the command processor.

batch   Specifies the batch file you wish to call as a subroutine.

To have control return to the first batch file and to have the secondary copy of the command processor unloaded, the EXIT command must be the last statement in the batch file used as a subroutine. If you do not place EXIT as the last command statement in the called batch file, control will not return to the calling batch file and the secondary copy of the command processor will continue to run.

Using The CALL Command

DOS 3.3 has added a CALL command that allows you to call a second batch file as a subroutine (that is, execute the commands in a second batch file without terminating the first batch file). This command can be used in place of the COMMAND and EXIT commands.

The syntax of the CALL command is

CALL *[d:][path]filename*

where

d:path   Specifies the name of the batch file to be
filename   called. When entering this file name, do not include the .BAT file extension.

You can use the CALL command to call its own batch file. However, you need to provide a method whereby the batch file is eventually terminated.

APPENDIX

The CONFIG.SYS File

Each time you boot up your computer, DOS searches the root directory of the drive from which it was started for a file named CONFIG.SYS. If this file is located, DOS executes all of the commands it contains much like a batch file (although this file is executed long before an AUTOEXEC.BAT file), according to the values assigned by special configuration commands. If DOS does not find this file in the root directory, it supplies its own default values for all of the configuration commands it requires.

The CONFIG.SYS file is used, then, only when you need to set new values for particular configuration commands. The parameters that can be modified in the CONFIG.SYS file include:

- The BREAK status
- The number of disk BUFFERS

- The COUNTRY specification
- Additional DEVICE drivers
- The maximum number of drives that you may access (LASTDRIVE)
- The maximum number of files that can be open concurrently by file handlers (FILES)
- The maximum number of files that can be open concurrently by file control blocks (FCBS)
- The SHELL
- Override the default stack resources (STACKS)

Each of these parameters is explained in this appendix, along with its associated commands.

Creating the CONFIG.SYS File

You can create the CONFIG.SYS file using the COPY command, EDLIN (the line editor supplied with DOS), or any other editor or word processor that can save its text in ASCII format. If you create it with a word processor, then save it in ASCII or text format and copy it to the root directory. To put the commands that you enter into commission, you must reboot your computer (Ctrl-Alt-Del, or turn the power off and on).

To create the CONFIG.SYS file using the COPY command, use the following model:

```
COPY   CON   CONFIG.SYS
```

Before creating a CONFIG.SYS file for a floppy or your hard disk, make sure that you are in the root directory (\) before you enter this command.

After typing this command and pressing the Enter key, you simply type in each configuration command to be processed when the CONFIG.SYS file is executed. After typing in each command, you terminate the line by pressing the Enter key.

Once you have entered all of the configuration command statements you wish to have in this file, you save it on disk (in the current directory) by pressing Ctrl-Z (you can also accomplish this by pressing F6 on IBM PCs and most compatibles) and the Enter key.

Controlling the BREAK Status

Normally, DOS checks for the BREAK key (Ctrl-Break) only when performing standard input/output or print operations because the default for the BREAK command is off. If you want DOS to check for the BREAK key under more circumstances, set the status to on by entering

BREAK = ON

as a line in the CONFIG.SYS file. Setting the status to on in this file will allow you to abort program operations that produce few or no standard device operations (such as running a compiler). For more information on the BREAK command, refer to its reference entry in the main text of the book.

The BUFFERS Parameter

A disk buffer is a specific block of RAM that DOS uses to store temporarily data that is being read or written to a disk. The default number of buffers maintained by DOS is 2. In version 3.3, the number of buffers is set according to these criteria:

- BUFFERS = 3 if you have a disk drive whose capacity is greater than 360K.
- BUFFERS = 5 if your computer has more than 128K RAM.
- BUFFERS = 10 if your computer has more than 256K RAM.
- BUFFERS = 15 if your computer has more than 512K RAM.

Only if none of these apply to your computer system is the default number of buffers set to 2. Each buffer that is added with the BUFFERS command uses up an additional 528 bytes of memory.

To open additional buffers, you use the BUFFERS command followed by the equal sign and the number of buffers to use in the CONFIG.SYS file. For example, to increase the number of buffers from 2 to 10, you would enter

BUFFERS = 10

in a line of the CONFIG.SYS file.

Generally, performance is enhanced when running application programs when you increase the number of buffers from the default of 2. However, there is a trade-off that can occur when you have somewhere between 10 and 20 buffers open (depending upon the type of application that you are using). At that point, it may take DOS as much time to locate data in a particular memory buffer as it would to get the data from disk.

Many DOS application programs, such as WordStar 2000 and dBASE III PLUS, require many more than 2 buffers in order to run. During installation of such software, the application's installation program checks the root directory to make sure first that the CONFIG.SYS exists and, if it does, to check the number of buffers open with the BUFFERS command. If the number is less than 20 (or the BUFFER command is not used in the file), the program will then automatically enter a BUFFERS command or edit an existing one to read as follows:

BUFFERS = 20

The COUNTRY Parameter

You can use the COUNTRY command in a CONFIG.SYS file to change the currency, date, or time format or the collating sequence to match that preferred by a foreign country. The syntax of the COUNTRY command is

COUNTRY = *xxx,[yyy],[d:]*COUNTRY.SYS

where

xxx	Specifies the country code (see SELECT).
yyy	Specifies the code page of the desired country

(in DOS 3.3, a country may have different information depending on the code page selected—see Appendix C of the DOS reference for a listing of the codes).

Note that if you have used the SELECT command, DOS will have already created a CONFIG.SYS file that includes the COUNTRY configuration command. To make changes to the COUNTRY codes, you must then edit the contents of this file using either EDLIN or a word processor that can read ASCII files.

Specifying Device Drivers

DOS automatically loads device drivers for standard input/output devices, printers, and storage devices such as floppy and fixed disk drives. Therefore, you need to use the DEVICE configuration command in the CONFIG.SYS file only when you need to install additional nonstandard devices (such as a mouse or an 8-inch floppy disk drive). The driver files for nonstandard devices are supplied by the device manufacturer.

To install a new device driver, you enter the DEVICE command followed by the equal sign and the name of the file that contains the driver on a line in the CONFIG.SYS file.

The DOS diskette includes two device drivers, ANSI.SYS and VDISK.SYS. Version 3.3 has added three more device drivers: DISPLAY.SYS, PRINTER.SYS, and DRIVER.SYS.

The ANSI.SYS Driver

The ANSI.SYS driver file extends cursor control and keyboard reassignments. These extended functions make it easier for software to control cursor positioning, display messages on the screen, set colors, and reassign keyboard functions. Some software applications, such as SuperKey, require that ANSI.SYS be loaded by the CONFIG.SYS file in order to run.

To add this driver, you enter

DEVICE = *[d:][path]***ANSI.SYS**

on a line of your CONFIG.SYS file, where

> *d:path*   Specifies the drive and path.

The VDISK.SYS Driver

The VDISK.SYS driver allows you to set up a virtual or RAM disk that performs the functions of a physical disk drive. A virtual disk, however, is installed in RAM and, therefore, disappears when power is interrupted to the computer system. You can install more than one virtual disk using the VDISK.SYS driver, depending upon the amount of RAM available to your system.

The syntax of the DEVICE configuration command when using the VDISK.SYS driver is as follows:

DEVICE = *[d:][path]***VDISK.SYS**   *[comment][bbb]*
[comment][sss][comment][ddd][/E[:m]]

Before explaining each optional parameter, consider the following example that uses all of the options:

DEVICE = **C:\DOS\VDISK.SYS**   **buffer size** = **256**
sector size = **512**   **directory entries** = **128 /E**

The options are as follows:

> *d:path*   Tells DOS where the VDISK.SYS file is located (C:\DOS in the example).
>
> *bbb*   Sets the size of the virtual disk in kilobytes. If you do not specify this parameter, DOS uses a default of 64K. You can enter a value between 1K and the amount of memory available to your computer. Notice that you can also add an optional *[comment]* explaining the value. In the example, the comment *buffer size=* precedes the value in kilobytes.
>
> *sss*   Sets the sector size in bytes. The default of 128 bytes is used by DOS if this parameter is omitted or an inaccurate value is entered. Allowable values for the sector size are 128, 256, or 512 bytes. The sector size parameter can also be preceded by an optional comment. In the

example, the comment *sector size*= has been added.

ddd   Sets the number of directory entries that the virtual disk can hold (one directory entry per file copied to the virtual disk). The default is 64, and you can enter a value between 2 and 512. However, DOS may automatically adjust the value you enter when installing the virtual disk. The value is increased to the nearest sector boundary (as set by the sector size). It is decreased if the size of the virtual disk (as set by the buffer size) is too small to accommodate the file allocation table, the directory, and two additional sectors. If the directory size reaches 1 and these files still cannot be accommodated, you will receive an error message and the virtual disk will not be installed.

comment   You may enter an optional comment before the *[ddd]* parameter. In the example, the comment *directory entries* = has been added.

/E   Tells DOS to install the virtual disk in extended memory (RAM at or beyond 1 megabyte). This parameter can only be used with a personal computer that has extended memory, such as the IBM PC AT or PS/2 machines (computers equipped with an add-on board such as the Intel Above Board support expanded instead of extended memory). When you add the /E parameter, the virtual disk buffer is established in extended memory while the device driver is installed in conventional memory. Extended memory up to 4 megabytes may be used for a single virtual disk.

:m   Specifies the maximum number of sectors (as specified by the *sss* parameter) of data that are transferred to the virtual disk at one time. The permissible values are 1 through 8, with 8 being the default value.

When a virtual disk is established in extended memory, interrupt servicing is suspended during data transfers. In some situations, this can result in some interrupts being lost. If this happens, you should install the virtual disk in conventional memory. If the problem is resolved, you can then resinstall the virtual disk in extended memory with a smaller *[:m]* value.

When you establish a virtual disk, DOS assigns it the next available drive letter specification. For example, if your computer has two floppy disk drives, A and B, the virtual disk will be given C as the drive letter specification. If you have a single fixed disk, C, the virtual disk will be given D as the drive letter specification.

The DISPLAY.SYS Driver

The DISPLAY.SYS device driver allows you to use code page switching on the EGA and IBM PS/2 displays and the IBM Convertible LCD screen. This device driver is included only in version 3.3 of DOS, which supports code page switching (see the CHCP and NLSFUNC command reference entries), and it is used only when you need to switch from the standard for U.S. symbols to new code pages containing international symbols.

The syntax of the DISPLAY.SYS DEVICE configuration command is as follows:

DEVICE = *[d:][path]***DISPLAY.SYS   CON[:]** = (*type[,[hwcp][,(n,m)]]*)

The options are as follows:

d:path	Specifies the drive letter and path that contain the DISPLAY.SYS file.
type	Specifies the display adapter type. You can use MONO, CGA, EGA, and LCD. Use EGA if you have an IBM PS/2 display (VGA is not yet fully supported).
hwcp	Specifies the code page. Permissible values are 437, 850, 860, 863, and 865 (refer to Appendix C of the DOS documentation for a description of these code page values).
n	Specifies the number of prepared code pages that can be supported. This must be a value

between 0 and 12 (refer to the table in the DOS documentation for the DISPLAY.SYS command to determine this value).

m   Specifies the number of subfonts supported by each code page (refer to the table in the DOS documentation for the DISPLAY.SYS command to determine this value).

Note that if you are using ANSI.SYS with DISPLAY.SYS, the DEVICE = ANSI.SYS statement must precede the configuration statement DEVICE = DISPLAY.SYS in the CONFIG.SYS file.

The PRINTER.SYS Driver

The PRINTER.SYS device driver allows you to use code page switching on the IBM Proprinter Model 4201 and the IBM Quietwriter III Model 5202. Like the DISPLAY.SYS file, this device driver is included only in version 3.3 of DOS, which supports code page switching (see the CHCP and NLSFUNC command reference entries), and it is used only when you need to switch from the standard for U.S. symbols to new code pages containing international symbols.

The syntax of the PRINTER.SYS DEVICE configuration command is as follows:

DEVICE = *[d:][path]***PRINTER.SYS**   **LPT**#*[:]* =
(*type[,[(hwcp1,hwcp2,...)][,n,]]*)

The options are as follows:

d:path   Specifies the drive letter and path that contain the PRINTER.SYS file.

LPT#   Specifies the printer device. It can be entered up to three times (for LPT1, LPT2, and LPT3). You can substitute PRN for LPT in the command line.

type   Specifies the type of printer use. You can choose between 4201 (IBM Proprinter) or 5202 (IBM Quietwriter III).

(*hwcp1,*
hwcp2,...)   Specifies the code page that is built into the hardware. The permissible values are 437,

850, 860, 863, and 865 (refer to the PRIN-
TER.SYS command in the DOS documentation for an explanation of how these code page
values are applied to the two printer types).

n   Specifies the number of additional code pages
that can be prepared. This value determines
the number of buffers that PRINTER.SYS
will set up to hold the code pages being prepared. The maximum number that can be
specified is 12.

The DRIVER.SYS Driver

The DRIVER.SYS statement in the CONFIG.SYS file allows you
to access and use a disk device by referring to a logical drive letter.
The syntax used when adding this to the CONFIG.SYS file is
as follows:

DEVICE = DRIVER.SYS   /D:*ddd*[/T:*ttt*][/S:*ss*][/H:*hh*]
[/C][/N][/F:*f*]

The options are as follows:

/D:*ddd*   Specifies the physical drive number between 0
and 255. The first physical diskette drive
(drive A) has the value 0. The second physical
diskette drive (drive B) has the value 1. The
third physical diskette drive (must be external)
has the value 2. The first fixed drive has the
value 128 and the second has the value 129.

/T:*ttt*   Specifies the number of tracks per side
between 1 and 999 (default: 80).

/S:*ss*   Specifies the number of sectors per track
between 1 and 99 (default: 9).

/H:*hh*   Specifies the number of drive heads between 1
and 99 (default: 2).

/C   Specifies that changeline support is required
(only used on computers such as the IBM PC
AT that support diskette changeline).

/N   Specifies that the physical device is a non-removable block device (such as a fixed disk).

/F:*f*   Specifies the device type (form factor). The value of the *f* parameter is determined as follows:

Device	Value
160K/180K	0
320K/360K	0
1.2 megabytes	1
720K or others	2
1.44 megabytes	7

Note that the DEVICE=DRIVER.SYS configuration statement is not used to drive fixed (hard) disks. To set a logical drive letter for a fixed disk, use the SUBST command (see the SUBST reference entry for more information).

To find out the logical drive letter assigned by DOS to the device driver for a particular computer configuration and value of /D:, refer to the table included in the DOS documentation under the reference entry for the DEVICE command.

The LASTDRIVE Parameter

The highest drive specification letter that DOS 3 will recognize is drive E (three fixed drives attached: C, D, and E). If your system has more than this number of logical or physical drives attached, you must add a LASTDRIVE statement to your CONFIG.SYS file:

LASTDRIVE = *x*

where

x   Specifies a letter between A and Z. If the drive letter you specify is less than the number of drives attached to your system, DOS will ignore the LASTDRIVE statement in the CONFIG.SYS file.

For example, if you are on a network and you have 15 drive volumes attached to the system, you would enter

LASTDRIVE = O

The FCBS Parameter

Some older application programs use file control blocks (FCBs) instead of the newer file handles to create, open, and delete files as well as to read from and write to files. When using these programs on a network with file sharing in use, you may have to increase the number of files that can be opened by FCBs. The default value used by DOS is 4 files.

To specify a new number of files that can be concurrently open by DOS, you use the FCBS command in the CONFIG.SYS file:

FCBS = x,y

where

x	Specifies the total number of files that can be opened by FCBs.
y	Specifies the number of files protected from automatic closure by DOS (the default is 0).

When file sharing is in use and an application program tries to open more than the total number of files, DOS closes the least-recently used file and opens the new file (excluding the files protected from automatic closure). If the program tries to read from or write to a file that has been closed by DOS, you will receive the following error message:

FCB unavailable
Abort, Fail?

To avoid such an error, you would add a FCBS command to your CONFIG.SYS file. For example, entering

FCBS = 10,5

would allow 10 FCB files to be open concurrently and would protect 5 of these from automatic closure.

When specifying the first parameter (the total number of FCB files), you can enter a value between 1 and 255. When specifying the second parameter (the number of files protected from automatic closure), you can enter a value between 0 and 255. (See also the SHARE command in the main text.)

The FILES Parameter

By default, DOS allows up to 8 files (controlled by file handles, not FCBs) to be open concurrently. This number is insufficient to run several newer application programs as well as some DOS commands (such as XCOPY).

If you receive either the error message

Too many open files

or

Too many files open

you will have to use the FILES configuration command in the CONFIG.SYS file to increase the maximum number of files available to the entire system:

FILES = n

where

n Specifies the number of files that can be opened at the same time (a value between 8 and 255). However, be aware that the maximum number of files that a single process can have opened is set at 20.

To accommodate 15 different files being open at one time, you would enter

FILES = 15

as a line in the CONFIG.SYS file.

The SHELL Parameter

Normally, DOS loads the command processor from the COM-MAND.COM file during the boot sequence. If you have your own command processor, you can have it initialized and loaded at start-up in place of COMMAND.COM by using the SHELL configuration command.

The syntax of the SHELL command is

SHELL = *[d:][path]filename* *[/E:xxxxx][/P]*

where

d:path filename	Specifies the file name of the new command processor (including its path, if it is not located in the root directory). Using COM-MAND.COM as the file name is a convenient way to increase the environment size under DOS 3.2 and 3.3.
/E:*xxxxx*	Specifies the number of bytes for the environment size (expressed as a base-10 integer between 160 and 32768).
/P	Causes COMMAND.COM to remain loaded and to execute the AUTOEXEC.BAT file (if one exists).

Note that using the SHELL command to run a different command processor does not affect the COMSPEC command, which points to the name of the controlling processor (see SET in the reference entries). If you use the SHELL command in the CON-FIG.SYS file to load a new command processor, you will also want to use the COMSPEC parameter in the SET command in the AUTOEXEC.BAT file to refer to it.

The STACKS Parameter

DOS 3.3 includes a STACKS configuration command that allows you to override the default stack resources used by DOS. The syntax of this command is

STACKS = *n,s*

where

n Specifies the number of stack frames between 8 and 64.

s Specifies the size in bytes of each stack frame between 32 and 512.

If the STACKS command is not included in the CONFIG.SYS file, the n and s parameters are set to 0 for the IBM PC, IBM PC XT, and the IBM Portable PC. For all other IBM personal computers, the default values are $n = 9$ and $s = 128$.

Every time a hardware interrupt occurs, DOS appropriates one stack frame from the stack pool. Once the interrupt has been processed, DOS returns the stack frame to the pool. If you experience stack overflow errors, you should use the STACKS command to increase the number of stack frames available to DOS.

APPENDIX

Partitioning Your Hard Disk

Hard disks are usually so large that they can contain more than one type of operating system. For example, you can have DOS 3.3 manage one part of a disk and UNIX manage another. Each of these sections is called a *partition*. You can have from one to four partitions on a disk.

Partitions are used to make the hard disk, especially a very large one, a more economical investment. They allow you to effectively have up to four completely different computer systems resident in one set of hardware. However, since they do not share a common software environment, they cannot share data directly.

Two types of partitions can be set up for DOS: a *primary DOS partition* and an *extended DOS partition*. The primary DOS partition is the partition that contains DOS and is the first partition on the disk. This is the only partition that must be on the disk if your disk is no larger than 32 megabytes. The extended DOS partition is a separate partition that cannot be used for booting, but can be divided into separate logical drives.

If you have more than 32 megabytes available on one hard disk, you will need to create an extended DOS partition, which is assigned the next logical drive letter. For example, if you had a 60-megabyte hard disk drive, and wanted access to all of it, you would create a 32-megabyte primary partition and a 28-megabyte extended partition. The primary partition could be accessed as drive C, while the extended partition would be called drive D. You could also subdivide the extended partition into more logical drives (up to the letter Z).

You must create partitions before using a hard disk drive. You will probably take the easiest route by simply making the entire disk into one primary partition. The FDISK program presented here, however, is necessary in several more advanced situations. For example, you may plan on using multiple operating systems from the same disk. FDISK will let you set up unique partitions for each system. (Each of these would be a primary partition, but only one could be designated the active partition, the one that will gain control at boot up.) Then again, you may be using one of the large hard disks (40 to 70 megabytes) that are increasingly common. Since DOS can only access a logical drive of 32 megabyte or less, you'll need to partition a larger physical drive into multiple logical drives. Only in this way can you store and retrieve information on the larger hard disk.

Note: If your disk is already being used and you wish to make a new partition, you will have to first back up all of your data and then run FDISK from a system diskette. Finally, you'll need to reformat your disk before restoring your files to it.

Configuring a DOS Partition

In this section, you will see exactly how to use the FDISK command. This procedure is very important, and it can have serious consequences if done incorrectly. However, it can also make your system more efficient, when done properly. FDISK is only usable on hard disk systems.

Invoking the FDISK command is as simple as typing

FDISK

and pressing Return. (Remember to have your path set properly to include the directory containing the FDISK command file.) After this command creates the appropriate partition(s), you must then logically format the disk.

Warning: All data on your disk will be destroyed when you create partitions with FDISK.

When you first execute FDISK, the screen will clear and the FDISK Options screen will appear. This contains the menu used to get around in FDISK (see Figure C.1).

As you can see, there are four choices. If you have a system with more than one hard disk drive, the number in the *Current Fixed Disk Drive: 1* line would be changed to the number of drives in your system. Also, a fifth option, *Select Next Fixed Disk Drive,* would be displayed on the screen. You can work on only one hard disk drive at a time, but you can switch from the drive you are working on to another drive. For now, let's assume you have one hard disk drive and that the screen in Figure C.1 is what you see.

Creating a Partition

The first option on the FDISK Options menu is to create a DOS partition. Since you are using DOS, and not another operating sys-

```
FDISK Options

Current Fixed Disk Drive: 1

Choose one of the following:

     1. Create DOS partition
     2. Change Active Partition
     3. Delete DOS partition
     4. Display Partition Information



Enter choice: [1]



Press ESC to return to DOS
```

Figure C.1: The FDISK Options menu

tem such as UNIX, you can only create DOS partitions. Should you wish to put another operating system onto the disk, that system would have its own version of FDISK and could then create its own partitions next to DOS'.

Tip: If you plan to use your hard disk to support another operating system, do not partition the whole disk. Leave some room so that another system can be loaded onto the disk.

Choosing the first option to create a DOS partition results in Figure C.2. If you select option 2 at this point, intending to create an extended DOS partition *before* creating a primary partition, DOS will display a message indicating that you cannot do so, and will suggest that you press Esc to return to the main FDISK Options menu. Assuming you are starting from scratch, you would select choice 1 to create the primary DOS partition. You will then see the screen shown in Figure C.3.

If you want to use the whole disk for DOS, then you answer Y on this screen. Doing so makes DOS use the whole disk. The computer will allocate the entire disk, and then come back with the message

System will now restart

Insert DOS diskette in drive A:
Press any key when ready . . .

```
Create DOS Partition

Current Fixed Disk Drive: 1


    1. Create Primary DOS partition
    2. Create Extended DOS partition




Enter choice: [1]



Press ESC to return to FDISK Options
```

Figure C.2: The Create DOS Partition menu

Since you just created the partition, there is still nothing on the hard disk. The system must be rebooted from the disk drive. You can now format the entire hard disk just as you would a floppy diskette.

If you answer N, as shown in Figure C.3, you have the opportunity to create a smaller partition, as shown in Figure C.4. As you can see, there are 305 *cylinders* available on the total disk. A hard disk consists of several platters, similar to a diskette; each platter consists of a series of concentric tracks made up of sectors. Each platter lies above another and is read by a different disk head. Viewed vertically, a series of tracks (with the same track number, but on different platters) located one above the other constitute a cylinder. The brackets in the screen shown in Figure C.4 indicate the place where you may enter a number for cylinders that is less than the default maximum (305 on this disk).

Notice that the second-to-last line on the screen tells you that no partitions have been defined yet. If you are using your disk for DOS alone, you should accept the default maximum cylinder value. All disk space will then be available for DOS and your DOS files. If you plan on splitting up your disk between DOS and another operating system, however, you'll have to decide for yourself what percentage of total disk space is needed for the other operating system. In this example, you

```
Create Primary DOS Partition

Current Fixed Disk Drive: 1

Do you wish to use the maximum size
for a DOS partition and make the DOS
partition active (Y/N).........? [n]




Press ESC to return to FDISK Options
```

Figure C.3: Creating the primary DOS partition

intend to create an extended DOS partition, so 200 was entered for the number of cylinders in the primary DOS partition.

Entering 200 results in the screen shown in Figure C.5. This screen tells you that the first partition on drive C is a primary DOS

```
Create Primary DOS Partition

Current Fixed Disk Drive: 1




Total disk space is  3Ø5 cylinders.
Maximum space available for partition
is  3Ø5 cylinders.

Enter partition size...........: [ 2ØØ]


No partitions defined

Press ESC to return to FDISK Options
```

Figure C.4: Defining the primary DOS partition's size

```
Create Primary DOS Partition

Current Fixed Disk Drive: 1

Partition Status   Type  Start  End Size
  C: 1             PRI DOS    Ø   199  2ØØ






Primary DOS partition created

Press ESC to return to FDISK Options ▪
```

Figure C.5: Primary DOS partition screen

partition (PRI DOS) that starts at cylinder 0 and ends at cylinder 199, constituting a total of 200 cylinders. Pressing Esc at this point returns you to the FDISK Options menu. If you again try to create a primary partition, DOS will show the following message on your screen:

Primary DOS partition already exists.
Press ESC to return to FDISK Options

Note: There can only be one primary DOS partition. When DOS boots up, the system files from this partition are loaded into memory for your operations. In this example, you have only used 200 cylinders out of a possible 305, so you can make an extended DOS partition. To do so, you select choice 1 on the FDISK Options menu (see Figure C.1) and then select choice 2 on the Create DOS Partition menu (see Figure C.2).

The resulting screen, shown in Figure C.6, allows you to create an extended DOS partition. This screen tells you the current partition information—that is, that there are 305 total cylinders available for use—and also tells you that 105 cylinders remain unused. The 105 value is used as the default entry at this stage. You only need to type in a number over the 105 to override the default. In Figure C.6, 55 was entered for the desired extended DOS partition, leaving 50 cylinders unused on the disk for another operating system.

```
Create Extended DOS Partition

Current Fixed Disk Drive: 1

Partition Status    Type  Start  End Size
  C: 1              PRI DOS    Ø   199  2ØØ




Total disk space is  3Ø5 cylinders.
Maximum space available for partition
is  1Ø5 cylinders.

Enter partition size...........: [  55]



Press ESC to return to FDISK Options
```

Figure C.6: Creating an extended DOS partition

The screen will now clear, redisplay the partition information (including that on the new extended DOS partition), and print the message

Extended DOS Partition created
Press ESC to return to FDISK Options

near the bottom of the screen. Pressing Esc will result in the next step of the process (see Figure C.7).

Since you have just created an extended DOS partition, DOS wants to know if you want to create logical drives within this new partition. It tells you the total available cylinders in the partition and asks you to enter a size for the logical drive. In this example, you enter 45. The resulting screen will contain the logical drive information (drive name, starting cylinder, ending cylinder, and total cylinders used).

Suppose you wanted to create another logical drive, E, using the remaining ten cylinders. You could again choose option 1 on the FDISK Options menu. You would go again to the Create DOS Partition menu, but there would be one new choice displayed:

3. Create logical DOS drive(s) in
the Extended DOS partition

```
  Create Logical DOS Drive(s)




  No logical drives defined


  Total partition size is    55 cylinders.

  Maximum space available for logical
  drive is    55 cylinders.

  Enter logical drive size........: [  45]


  Press ESC to return to FDISK Options
```

Figure C.7: Defining logical drives

This would bring you back to the screen for defining logical drives, where you could then enter the information for drive E. Going through this same sequence again in order to use the remaining ten cylinders will result in Figure C.8. Notice that the cylinder numbers are within the bounds of the extended DOS partition. You are told that DOS created two logical drives, D and E, with sizes of 45 and 10 cylinders. Furthermore, you're reminded that no more available space remains for any other logical drives. Press Esc, and you will once again be back at the FDISK Options menu.

If you try to create another extended partition, you will get a partition information screen and the message

Extended DOS partition already exists.
Press ESC to return to FDISK Options

Changing the Active Partition

The *active* partition is the partition that is used to boot the system. It is the default partition. Choosing option 2 on the main FDISK Options menu leads you to a menu like that shown in Figure C.9, in which the partition information is displayed along with the total number of cylinders available on the disk. FDISK now wants to know the number of the partition that you wish to make active.

```
    Create Logical DOS Drive(s)

    Drv Start End  Size
     D:  200   244   45
     E:  245   254   10












    All available space in the Extended DOS
    partition is assigned to logical drives.


    Logical DOS drive created, drive letters
    changed or added
    Press ESC to return to FDISK Options _
```

Figure C.8: Logical drive summary screen

If you enter the number 2, as shown in the figure, DOS will inform you that only the primary DOS partition (1) may be made active. Type the number 1 so that the primary DOS partition will have control when the system comes up. Pressing Return will result in the adjusted partition information display seen in Figure C.10.

```
Change Active Partition

Current Fixed Disk Drive: 1

Partition Status    Type  Start  End Size
  C: 1              PRI DOS    Ø  199  2ØØ
     2              EXT DOS  2ØØ  254   55


Total disk space is  3Ø5 cylinders.

Enter the number of the partition you
want to make active...............: [2]



Partition selected (2) is not bootable,
active partition not changed.
Press ESC to return to FDISK Options
```

Figure C.9: The Change Active Partition menu

```
Change Active Partition

Current Fixed Disk Drive: 1

Partition Status    Type  Start  End Size
  C: 1         A    PRI DOS    Ø  199  2ØØ
     2              EXT DOS  2ØØ  254   55


Total disk space is  3Ø5 cylinders.




Partition 1 made active

Press ESC to return to FDISK Options ▪
```

Figure C.10: Display of the active partition

Notice the letter A on the first line of this display. An A under *Status* tells you that partition 1 is the active partition. Pressing Esc takes you back to the FDISK Options menu.

Displaying Partition Information

Option 4 on the FDISK Options menu is used to display information about the partitions. This is useful because no extra functions will be executed at the same time; you can simply look at the information. Choosing option 4 yields the screen shown in Figure C.11.

The information at the top of the screen is familiar by now. But what if you want to see information about the logical drives that have been defined? Look at the bottom half of the screen, where you are asked if you want to see this information. Replying with Y results in a display of information about these logical drives (see Figure C.12). Pressing Esc at this point will return you to the FDISK Options menu.

Deleting DOS Partitions

As with most things, what DOS giveth, DOS can taketh away—with a little prodding from you. Selecting choice 3 on the FDISK

```
Display Partition Information

Current Fixed Disk Drive: 1

Partition Status    Type  Start  End Size
  C: 1        A    PRI DOS     0  199  200
     2             EXT DOS   200  254   55


Total disk space is  305 cylinders.


The Extended DOS partition contains
logical DOS drives. Do you want to
display logical drive information?  [Y]


Press ESC to return to FDISK Options
```

Figure C.11: Displaying partition information

Options menu produces the Delete DOS Partition menu, shown in Figure C.13.

Using this menu, you can delete any of the information you've already set up. You may want to expand or contract other partitions,

```
Display Logical DOS Drive Information

Drv Start End  Size
 D:  200   244   45
 E:  245   254   10




Press ESC to return to FDISK Options ▪
```

Figure C.12: Logical drive information

```
Delete DOS Partition

Current Fixed Disk Drive: 1

Choose one of the following:

    1.  Delete Primary DOS partition
    2.  Delete Extended DOS partition
    3.  Delete logical DOS drive(s) in
        the Extended DOS Partition


Enter choice: [ ]



Press ESC to return to FDISK Options ▪
```

Figure C.13: The Delete DOS Partition menu

or you may no longer want to use a partition in the manner you originally designed. In any case, you can only make changes in a certain
order. You cannot delete the primary DOS partition without first
deleting the extended DOS partition. If you try, DOS will give you
this message:

**Cannot delete Primary DOS partition on
drive 1 when Extended partition exists**

Press ESC to return to FDISK Options

In addition, you cannot delete an extended DOS partition without
first "undefining" (deleting) the logical drives in that partition. Trying to delete the extended DOS partition before deleting the drives
in it will simply display the current partition information with the
patient message

**Cannot delete Extended DOS partition
while logical drives exist.
Press ESC to return to FDISK options**

Choice 3 in the Delete DOS Partition menu is probably the first
selection you will need to make; you work your way backwards

```
    Delete Logical DOS Drive

    Drv  Start  End   Size
     D:   200   244    45
     E:   245   254    10




    Total partition size is    55 cylinders.

    Warning! Data in the logical DOS drive
    will be lost. What drive do you wish
    to delete........................? [e]

    Are you sure....................? [y]

    Press ESC to return to FDISK Options
```

Figure C.14: Deleting a logical drive

through the order in which you created things. (Actually, you will find that this is a fairly natural process.) Selecting choice 3 produces the screen shown in Figure C.14, which contains the logical drive information and the size of the extended DOS partition the drives are in. You are also warned that any data contained in the logical disk drive to be deleted will also be deleted.

If you still want to delete the drive, simply enter the drive identifier. You will then be asked to confirm this step. In Figure C.14, you have selected drive E to delete first, and confirmed the choice by typing Y. If you had entered N, you would have been returned to the FDISK Options menu.

Once FDISK deletes the logical drive, it updates the display at the top of the screen and asks for another drive to delete. If you wanted to regain all the space used by this partition, you would then enter drive D, confirm your entry, and end up with the screen shown in Figure C.15. Pressing Esc twice at this point would bring you back up through the menu screens to the main FDISK Options menu.

Now that the logical drives are gone, you can delete the extended DOS partition itself if you choose to do so. Choosing option 2 on the Delete DOS Partition menu results in the familiar form of an FDISK screen (see Figure C.16). Again, you are shown the partition information display (as in Figure C.11), warned that data will be

```
    Delete Logical DOS Drive

    Drv Start End  Size
     D: drive deleted
     E: drive deleted




    Total partition size is   55 cylinders.
    All logical drives deleted in the
    Extended DOS partition



    Press ESC to return to FDISK Options ▪
```

Figure C.15: Summary of logical drive deletions

lost, and asked if you really want to delete the extended DOS partition. If you reply Y, the screen will be updated to show only the primary DOS partition and the message

Extended DOS partition deleted

Press ESC to return to FDISK Options

Press Esc to return once again to the FDISK Options menu.

```
Delete Extended DOS Partition

Current Fixed Disk Drive: 1

Partition Status   Type  Start  End Size
  C: 1        A    PRI DOS    Ø   199  2ØØ
     2             EXT DOS  2ØØ   254   55




Warning! Data in the Extended DOS
partition will be lost. Do you wish
to continue.....................? [y]


Press ESC to return to FDISK Options
```

Figure C.16: Deleting the extended DOS partition

APPENDIX

Glossary

This appendix defines all of the important DOS-related terms you may encounter in this book or elsewhere in the literature.

active partition   The section of a hard disk containing the operating system to be used when the hardware powers up.

ANSI driver   A device driver, contained in the ANSI.SYS file, that loads additional support for advanced console features.

application program   A program that performs or replaces a manual function, such as balancing a checkbook or managing inventory.

archive bit   A bit in a file specification used to indicate whether the file in question needs to be backed up.

ASCII   American Standard Code for Information Interchange. The coding scheme whereby every character the computer can access is assigned an integer code between 0 and 255.

assembly language   A symbolic form of computer language used to program computers at a fundamental level.

asynchronous communications   *See* serial communications.

AUTOEXEC.BAT   A batch file executed automatically whenever the computer is booted up.

background task   A second program running on your computer; usually, a printing operation that shares the CPU with your main foreground task.

base name   The portion of a file name to the left of the period separator; it can be up to eight characters long.

BASIC   Beginner's All-purpose Symbolic Instruction Code. A computer language similar to the English language.

batch file   An ASCII file containing a sequence of DOS commands that, when invoked, will assume control of the computer, executing the commands as if they were entered successively by a computer user.

baud rate   The speed of data transmission, usually in bits per second.

binary   A numbering system that uses powers of 2 to generate all other numbers.

bit   One-eighth of a byte. A bit is a binary digit, either 0 or 1.

bit mapping   The way a graphics screen is represented in the computer. Usually signifies point-to-point graphics.

booting up   *See* bootstrapping.

boot record   The section on a disk that contains the minimum information DOS needs to start the system.

bootstrapping   When the computer initially is turned on or is rebooted from the keyboard with Ctrl-Alt-Del, it "pulls itself up by its bootstraps." *See also* warm booting, cold booting.

branching   The transfer of control or execution to another statement in a batch file. *See also* decision making.

Break key   The control-key combination that interrupts an executing program or command; activated by pressing the Scroll Lock/Break key while holding down the Ctrl key.

buffer   An area in memory set aside to speed up the transfer of data, allowing blocks of data to be transferred at once.

byte   The main unit of memory in a computer. A byte is an 8-bit binary-digit number. One character usually takes up one byte.

cache   A portion of memory reserved for the contents of recently referenced disk sectors. Facilitates faster reaccess of the same sectors.

case sensitivity   Distinguishing between capital letters and lowercase letters.

chaining   Passing the control of execution from one batch file to another. This represents an unconditional transfer of control.

character set   A complete group of 256 characters that can be used by programs or system devices. Consists of letters, numbers, control codes, and special graphics or international symbols. *See also* code page.

cluster   A group of contiguous sectors on a disk. This is the smallest unit of disk storage that DOS can manipulate.

COBOL   A programming language usually used for business applications.

code page   A character set that redefines the country and keyboard information for non–U.S. keyboards and systems.

cold booting   When the computer's power is first turned on and DOS first boots up. *See* bootstrapping.

COMMAND.COM   The command processor that comes with DOS.

command line   The line on which a command is entered. This line contains the command and all of its associated parameters and switches. It may run to more than one screen line, but it is still one command line.

command processor   The program that translates and acts on commands.

compressed print   Printing that allows more than 80 characters on a line of output (usually 132 characters, but on newer printers up to 255 characters per line).

computer-aided design (CAD) program A sophisticated software package containing advanced graphics and drawing features. Used by engineers, architects, and designers for drawing and design applications.

concatenation The placing of two or more text files together in a series.

conditional statement A statement in a batch file that controls the next step to be executed in the batch file, based on the value of a logical test.

CONFIG.SYS An ASCII text file containing system configuration commands.

configuration An initial set of system values, such as the number of buffers DOS will use, the number of simultaneously open files it will allow, and the specific devices that will be supported.

console The combination of your system's monitor and keyboard.

contiguity That the disk sectors used by a file are physically adjacent on a disk.

control codes ASCII codes that do not display a character but perform a function, such as ringing a bell or deleting a character.

copy protection Special mechanisms contained in diskettes to inhibit the copying of them by conventional commands.

CPU Central Processing Unit. The main chip that executes all individual computer instructions.

Ctrl-Z The end-of-file marker.

cursor The blinking line or highlighted box that indicates where the next keystroke will be displayed or what the next control code entered will affect.

cutting and pasting Selecting text from one part of a document or visual display and moving it to another location.

cylinder Two tracks that are in the same place on different sides of a double-sided disk. May be extended to include multiple platters. For example, Side 0 Track 30, Side 1 Track 30, Side 2 Track 30, and Side 3 Track 30 form a cylinder.

daisy-wheel printer A printer that uses circular templates for producing letter-quality characters.

data area   The tracks on a disk that contain user data.

database   A collection of data organized into various categories. A phone book is one form of database.

database management system   A software program designed to allow the creation of specially organized files, as well as data entry, manipulation, removal, and reporting for those files.

data bits   The bits that represent data when the computer is communicating.

data disk   A disk that has been formatted without the /S switch. The disk can contain only data; no room has been reserved for system files.

data stream   The transmission of data between two components or computers.

dead key   A reserved key combination on international keyboards, which outputs nothing itself but allows the next keystroke to produce an accent mark above or below the keystroke's usual character.

debugging   The process of discovering what is wrong with a program, where the problem is located, and what the solution is.

decimal   A numbering system based on ten digits.

decision making   A point in a batch file at which execution can continue on at least two different paths, depending on the results of a program test. Also known as logical testing or branching.

default   The standard value of a variable or system parameter.

deferred execution   In a program or batch file, when execution is delayed until a value for some parameter is finally entered or computed.

delimiter   A special character, such as a comma or space, used to separate values or data entries.

destination   The targeted location for data, files, or other information generated or moved by a DOS command.

device   Any internal or external piece of peripheral hardware.

device driver   Also known as an interrupt handler. A special program that must be loaded to use a device. Adds extra capability to DOS.

device name Logical name that DOS uses to refer to a device.

digital A representation based on a collection of individual digits, such as 0s and 1s in the binary number system.

digitizer A device with a movable arm that can take an image and break it up into small parts, which the computer translates into bits.

directory A grouping of files on a disk. These files are displayed together and may include access to other directories (subdirectories).

directory tree The treelike structure created when a root directory has several subdirectories, each of the subdirectories has subdirectories, and so on.

disk drive A hardware device that accesses the data stored on a disk.

diskette A flexible, oxide-coated disk used to store data. Also called a floppy diskette.

disk optimizer A program that rearranges the location of files stored on a disk in order to make the data in those files quickly retrievable.

DOS Disk Operating System. A disk manager and the program that allows computer/user interaction.

DOS environment A part of memory set aside to hold the defaults needed in the current environment, such as COMSPEC, PATH, LASTDRIVE, and so on.

DOS prompt Usually C> or A>. The visual indication that DOS is waiting for a command or prompting you for input.

dot-matrix printer A printer that represents characters by means of tiny dots.

double-density diskette A diskette on which magnetic storage material is arranged twice as densely as usual, allowing the storage of twice the usual amount of data. Generally refers to a 360K, 5¼-inch diskette.

drive identifier A single letter assigned to represent a drive, such as drive A or drive B. Usually requires a colon after it, such as A:.

DRIVER.SYS A file containing a device driver for an extra external disk drive. Used in the CONFIG.SYS file.

dual tasking   Causing two tasks or programming events to occur simultaneously.

echoing   Displaying on your video monitor the keystrokes you type in.

EDLIN   The DOS line editor.

end-of-file marker   A Ctrl-Z code that marks the logical end of a file.

environment   The context within which DOS interfaces with you and with your commands.

error level   A code, set by programs as they conclude processing, that tells DOS whether an error occurred, and if so, the severity of that error.

expansion cards   Add-on circuit boards through which hardware can increase the power of the system, such as adding extra memory or a modem.

expansion slots   Connectors inside the computer in which expansion cards are placed so that they tie in directly to the system.

extended ASCII codes   ASCII codes between 128 and 255, which usually differ from computer to computer.

extended DOS partition   A hard-disk partition used to exceed the 32 megabyte, single-disk barrier; it can be divided into logical disk drives.

extended memory   Additional physical memory beyond the DOS 1 megabyte addressing limit.

extension   The one to three characters after the period following the base name in a file specification.

external buffer   A device, connected to the computer and another device, that acts as a buffer.

file   A collection of bytes, representing a program or data, organized into records and stored as a named group on a disk.

file allocation table (FAT)   A table of sectors stored on a disk, which tells DOS whether a given sector is good, bad, continued, or the end of a chain of records.

file name   The name of a file on the disk. Usually refers to the base name, but can include the extension as well.

file version   A term that refers to which developmental copy of a software program is being used or referenced.

filter   A program that accepts data as input, processes it in some manner, and then outputs the data in a different form.

fixed disk   IBM's name for a hard disk.

floppy diskette   *See* diskette.

flow of control   The order of execution of batch file commands; how the control flows from one command to another, even when the next command to be executed is not located sequentially in the file.

foreground task   The main program running on your computer, as opposed to the less visible background task (usually a printing job).

formatting   The placement of timing marks on a disk to arrange the tracks and sectors for subsequent reading and writing.

fragmentation   A condition in which many different files have been stored in noncontiguous sectors on a disk.

function keys   Special-purpose keys on a keyboard, which can be assigned unique tasks by DOS or by application programs.

global characters   *See* wildcards.

graphics mode   The mode in which all screen pixels on a monitor are addressable and can be used to generate detailed images. Contrasts with text mode, which usually allows only 24 lines of 80 characters.

hard disk   A rigid platter that stores data faster and at a higher density than a floppy diskette. Sealed in an airtight compartment to avoid contaminants that could damage or destroy the disk.

hardware   The physical components of a computer system.

hardware interrupt   A signal from a device to the computer, indicating that an event has taken place.

head   A disk-drive mechanism that reads data from and writes data to the disk.

head crash   Occurs when the head hits the disk platter on a hard disk, physically damaging the disk and the data on it.

help file   A file of textual information containing helpful explanations of commands, modes, and other on-screen tutorial information.

hexadecimal   A numbering system in base 16. A single 8-bit byte can be fully represented as two hexadecimal digits.

hidden files   Files whose names do not appear in a directory listing. Usually refers to DOS' internal system files, but can also refer to certain files used in copy-protection schemes.

high-capacity diskette   A 1.2 megabyte, 5-1/4-inch floppy diskette.

high-resolution mode   The mode on a video monitor in which all available pixels are used to provide the most detailed screen image possible. On a color monitor, this mode reduces the possible range of colors that can be output.

horizontal landscape   When output to a printer is not done in the usual format, but rather with the wider part of the paper laid out horizontally, as in a landscape picture.

hot key   A key combination used to signal that a memory-resident program should begin operation.

housekeeping   Making sure the directory stays intact and well organized, and that unnecessary files are deleted.

hub   The center hole of a diskette.

IF   A conditional statement in a batch file.

ink-jet printer   A printer that forms characters by spraying ink in a dot pattern. *See* dot-matrix printer.

interface   The boundary between two things, such as the computer and a peripheral.

interrupt   A signal sent to the computer from a hardware device, indicating a request for service or support from the system.

keyboard translation table   An internal table, contained in the keyboard driver, that converts hardware signals from the keyboard into the correct ASCII codes.

key combination   When two or more keys are pressed simultaneously, as in Ctrl-Scroll Lock or Ctrl-Alt-Del.

key redefinition   Assigning a nonstandard value to a key.

kilobyte (K)   1024 bytes.

laser printer   A printer that produces images (pictures or text) by shining a laser on a photostatic drum, which picks up toner and then transfers the image to paper.

LCD   Liquid Crystal Display. A method of producing an image using electrically sensitive crystals suspended in a liquid medium.

letter-quality printer   A printer that forms characters that are comparable to those of a typewriter.

line editor   A program that can make textual changes to an ASCII file, but can only make changes to one line of the file at a time.

line feed   When the cursor on a screen moves to the next line, or when the print head on a printer moves down the paper to the next line.

literal   Something that is accepted exactly as it was submitted.

lockup   Occurs when the computer will not accept any input and may have stopped processing. Requires that the computer be warm or cold booted to resume operating.

log file   A separate file, created with the BACKUP command, that keeps track of the names of all files written to the backup diskette(s).

logging on   Signing onto a remote system, such as a mainframe or telecommunications service.

logical   Something that is defined based on a decision, not by physical properties.

logical drives   Disk drives, created in an extended DOS partition, that do not physically exist, but DOS operates as if they do. A means for DOS to access a physical disk that has more than 32 megabytes available.

logical testing   *See* decision making.

machine language   The most fundamental way to program a computer, using instructions made up entirely of strings of 0s and 1s.

macro   A set of commands, often memory-resident. When executed, they appear to the program executing them as if they were being entered by you.

medium-resolution mode   The mode on a Color Graphics Adapter in which only 320 × 200 pixels of resolution are allowed.

megabyte (Mb)   1024 kilobytes.

memory   The circuitry in a computer that stores information. *See also* RAM and ROM.

memory-resident   Located in physical memory, as opposed to being stored in a disk file.

menu   A set of choices displayed in tabular format.

meta symbols   Special single-character codes used by the PROMPT command to represent complex actions or sequences to be included in the DOS prompt.

microfloppy diskette   The 3½-inch diskette format used in the new PS/2 and many other computers.

modem   A device that transmits digital data in tones over a phone line.

monitor   The device used to display images; a display screen.

monochrome   Using two colors only: the background and foreground.

mouse   A device that moves the screen cursor by means of a hand-held apparatus moved along a surface such as a desk. The computer can tell how far and in which direction the mouse is being moved.

multitasking   When two or more computing applications are executing simultaneously.

national language-support operations   The DOS 3.3 feature that supports displays and printers, using a new range of code and character groupings.

network   Several computers, connected together, that can share common data files and peripheral devices.

nibble   Four bits, or half a byte.

octal   A numbering system in base 8.

operating system   *See* DOS.

overlay files   Files containing additional command and control information for sophisticated and complex programs. An overlay file is usually too large to fit into memory along with the main .EXE or .COM file.

overwriting   Typing new data over what is already there.

parallel communications   Data transmission in which several bits can be transferred or processed at one time.

parameter   An extra bit of information, specified with a command, that determines how the command executes.

parity bit   The bit, added to the end of a stream of data bits, that makes the total of the data bits and the parity bits odd or even.

partition   The section of a hard disk that contains an operating system. There can be at most four partitions on one hard disk.

Pascal   A programming language used mainly in computer science.

password   A sequence of characters that allows entry into a restricted system or program.

path   The list of disks and directories that DOS will search through to find a command file ending in .COM, .BAT, or .EXE.

peripheral   Any physical device connected to the computer.

piping   Redirecting the input or output of one program or command to another program or command.

pixel   The smallest unit of display on a video monitor—in short, a dot—that can be illuminated to create text or graphics images.

platter   The rigid disk used in a hard disk drive.

plotter   A device that draws data on paper with a mechanical arm.

port   A doorway through which the computer can access external devices.

primary DOS partition   Up to the first 32 megabytes of a hard disk. Contains the boot record and other DOS information files.

printer   A device that outputs data onto paper using pins (dot matrix), a daisy wheel, ink jets, laser imaging, and so on.

public domain   Something not copyrighted or patented. Public domain software can be used and copied without infringing on anyone's rights.

queue   A series of files waiting in line to be printed.

RAM   Random Access Memory. The part of the computer's memory to which you have access; stores programs and data while the computer is on.

RAM disk   An area of RAM that acts as if it were a disk drive. All data in this area of memory is lost when the computer is turned off or warm booted. Also known as a virtual disk.

range   A contiguous series of values (minimum to maximum, first to last, and so on).

read-after-write verification   An extra level of validity checking, invoked with the VERIFY command or the /V switch. Rereads data after writing it to disk, comparing the written data to the original information.

read-only status   Indicates that a file cannot be updated but can be read.

read/write bit   The bit in a file specification that indicates whether a file can accept changes or deletions, or can only be accessed for reading.

redirection   Causing output from one program or device to be routed to another program or device.

REM statement   A line in a BASIC program containing remarks or comments for program explanation or clarification.

reserved names   Specific words, in a programming language or operating system, that should not be used in any other application context.

resident commands   Commands located in random access memory.

resource allocation   Making system facilities available to individual users or programs.

reverse video   Black letters on a white background.

ROM   Read-Only Memory. The section of memory that you can only read from. This contains the basic computer operating system and system routines.

root directory   The first directory on any disk.

scan code   The hardware code representing a key pressed on a keyboard. Converted by a keyboard driver into an ASCII code for use by DOS and application programs.

scrolling   What the screen does when you're at the bottom of it and press Return—all of the lines roll up.

secondary command processor   A second copy of COM-MAND.COM, invoked either to run a batch file or to provide a new context for subsequent DOS commands.

sector   A division of a disk track; usually, 512 bytes.

serial communications   Data transmission in which data is transferred and processed one bit at a time. Also known as asynchronous communications.

shareware   Public domain software. *See also* public domain.

snapshot program   A program used in debugging to store the status of system or application program variables.

software   The programs and instruction sets that operate the computer.

software interrupt   A signal from a software program that calls up a routine that is resident in the computer's basic programming. Also, a software signal to the computer that the software program has finished, has a problem, and so on.

source   The location containing the original data, files, or other information to be used in a DOS command.

spooling   Simultaneous Peripheral Operations On-Line. Using a high-speed disk to store input to or output from low-speed peripheral devices while the CPU does other tasks.

spreadsheet program   An electronic version of an accountant's spreadsheet; when one value changes, all other values based on that value are updated instantly.

start bit   The bit sent at the beginning of a data stream to indicate that data bits follow.

stop bit   The bit sent after the data bits, indicating that no more data bits follow.

string   A series of characters.

subcommands   Several special commands used only within batch files.

subdirectory   A directory contained within another directory or subdirectory. Technically, all directories other than the root directory are subdirectories.

switch   A parameter included in DOS commands, usually preceded by the slash (/) symbol, that clarifies or modifies the action of the command.

synchronization   The coordination of a sending and receiving device, so that both simultaneously send and receive data at the same rate.

system disk   A disk containing the necessary DOS files for system booting.

text mode   The mode in which standard characters can be displayed on a monitor.

time slice   The smallest unit of time managed and assigned by the operating system to programs and other processing activities.

toggle   A switch or command that reverses a value from off to on, or from on to off.

track   A circular stream of data on the disk. Similar to a track on a record, only not spiraling.

transient command   A command whose procedures are read from the disk into memory, executed from memory, and then erased from memory when finished.

utility   A supplemental routine or program designed to carry out a specific operation, usually to modify the system environment or perform housekeeping tasks.

variable parameter   A named element, following a command, that acts as a placeholder; when you issue the command, you replace the variable parameter with the actual value you want to use.

verbose listing   A listing of all files and subdirectories contained on the disk and path specified in the command. Activated by the CHKDSK command with the /V switch.

vertical portrait   The conventional $8\frac{1}{2}$-by-11-inch output for printed information, with the long side of the paper positioned vertically.

virtual disk   *See* RAM disk.

volume label   A name, consisting of up to 11 characters, that can be assigned to any disk during a FORMAT operation or after formatting with the LABEL command.

warm booting   Resetting the computer using the Ctrl-Alt-Del key combination. *See* bootstrapping.

wide directory listing   An alternate output format that lists four columns of file names.

wildcards   Characters used to represent any other characters. In DOS, ★ and ? are the only wildcard symbols.

word processor   A computerized typewriter. Allows the correction and reformatting of documents before they are printed.

write-protection   Giving a disk read-only status by covering the write-protect notch.

APPENDIX

ASCII Codes

This appendix presents information on how ASCII codes are created, used, and manipulated in DOS. It discusses the different numbering systems used to create these codes, as well as how codes are grouped to form identifiable character sets. Using this information, you can both manage your system more readily and manipulate file data for yourself.

Character Sets

Just as you use an alphabet and a decimal numbering system, the computer uses its own character and numbering system. DOS maintains, in memory, all of the characters of the English alphabet, including numbers and symbols, as well as some foreign symbols (such as accented vowels). This group of symbols is called a character set. By changing the symbols in this set, you can obtain completely new character sets. This is especially useful for people living in other countries, who have less daily need of U.S. standard characters and who would rather work with their own characters.

ASCII Codes

A character is any letter, number, punctuation symbol, or graphics symbol. In other words, it is anything that can be displayed on a video screen or printed on a printer.

Each character in a character set has a number assigned to it, which is how the computer refers to the various characters in the set. For example, code 65 refers to a capital A, and code 97 refers to a lowercase a. These codes are called ASCII codes (pronounced "*ask-ee* codes"); ASCII stands for American Standard Code for Information Interchange.

Codes 0 through 31 are used as control codes. Displaying one of these codes will cause something to happen instead of causing a symbol to be displayed. For example, displaying code 7 will result in the computer's bell or beeper being sounded. Displaying code 13 will result in a carriage return.

Codes 32 through 127 are ASCII character codes for numbers, letters, and all punctuation marks and symbols. Codes 128 through 255, known as extended ASCII codes, vary from computer to computer. They usually comprise foreign characters, Greek and mathematical symbols, and graphics characters. (Graphics characters consist of small lines and curves that can be used to create geometric patterns.)

DOS 3.3 has several available ASCII tables, called code pages. The most common is the standard U.S. code page (see Table E.1); the next most common is the Multilingual code page (see Table E.2).

Mapping One Character Set onto Another

Any device that displays characters has a device driver that literally drives, or controls, the device. When the computer tells a printer to

HEX DIGITS 1st 2nd	0-	1-	2-	3-	4-	5-	6-	7-	8-	9-	A-	B-	C-	D-	E-	F-
0-		►		0	@	P	`	p	Ç	É	á	▓	└	╨	α	≡
1-	☺	◄	!	1	A	Q	a	q	ü	æ	í	▓	┴	╤	β	±
2-	●	↕	"	2	B	R	b	r	é	Æ	ó	▓	┬	╥	Γ	≥
3-	♥	‼	#	3	C	S	c	s	â	ô	ú	│	├	╙	π	≤
4-	♦	¶	$	4	D	T	d	t	ä	ö	ñ	┤	─	╘	Σ	⌠
5-	♣	§	%	5	E	U	e	u	à	ò	Ñ	╡	┼	╒	σ	⌡
6-	♠	▬	&	6	F	V	f	v	å	û	ª	╢	╞	╓	µ	÷
7-	•	↨	'	7	G	W	g	w	ç	ù	º	╖	╟	╫	τ	≈
8-	◘	↑	(	8	H	X	h	x	ê	ÿ	¿	╕	╚	╪	Φ	°
9-	○	↓	)	9	I	Y	i	y	ë	Ö	⌐	╣	╔	┘	Θ	∙
A-	◎	→	*	:	J	Z	j	z	è	Ü	¬	║	╩	┌	Ω	·
B-	♂	←	+	;	K	[	k	{	ï	¢	½	╗	╦	█	δ	√
C-	♀	∟	,	<	L	\	l			î	£	¼	╝	╠	▄	∞	ⁿ
D-	♪	↔	-	=	M	]	m	}	ì	¥	¡	╜	═	▌	φ	²
E-	♫	▲	.	>	N	^	n	~	Ä	Pt	«	╛	╬	▐	ε	■
F-	☼	▼	/	?	O	_	o	△	Å	ƒ	»	┐	╧	▀	∩	

Table E.1: U.S. ASCII table (code page 437 in DOS 3.3)

HEX DIGITS 1st 2nd	0-	1-	2-	3-	4-	5-	6-	7-	8-	9-	A-	B-	C-	D-	E-	F-
0-		►		0	@	P	`	p	Ç	É	á	▓	└	ð	Ó	-
1-	☺	◄	!	1	A	Q	a	q	ü	æ	í	▓	┴	Ð	ß	±
2-	●	↕	"	2	B	R	b	r	é	Æ	ó	▓	┬	Ê	Ô	‗
3-	♥	‼	#	3	C	S	c	s	â	ô	ú	│	├	Ë	Ò	¾
4-	♦	¶	$	4	D	T	d	t	ä	ö	ñ	┤	─	È	õ	¶
5-	♣	§	%	5	E	U	e	u	à	ò	Ñ	Á	┼	ı	Õ	§
6-	♠	▬	&	6	F	V	f	v	å	û	ª	Â	ã	Í	µ	÷
7-	•	↨	'	7	G	W	g	w	ç	ù	º	À	Ã	Î	þ	¸
8-	◘	↑	(	8	H	X	h	x	ê	ÿ	¿	©	╚	Ï	Þ	°
9-	○	↓	)	9	I	Y	i	y	ë	Ö	®	╣	╔	┘	Ú	¨
A-	◎	→	*	:	J	Z	j	z	è	Ü	¬	║	╩	┌	Û	·
B-	♂	←	+	;	K	[	k	{	ï	ø	½	╗	╦	█	Ù	¹
C-	♀	∟	,	<	L	\	l			î	£	¼	╝	╠	▄	ý	³
D-	♪	↔	-	=	M	]	m	}	ì	Ø	¡	¢	═	¦	Ý	²
E-	♫	▲	.	>	N	^	n	~	Ä	×	«	¥	╬	Ì	¯	■
F-	☼	▼	/	?	O	_	o	△	Å	ƒ	»	┐	¤	▀	´	

Table E.2: Multilingual ASCII table (code page 850 in DOS 3.3)

print the letter A, DOS sends the code 65 to the printer driver, which converts the 65 into a series of control codes that will print the A.

For the sake of consistency, computers, printers, and displays all have the same character sets and coding system for ASCII codes 32 through 127. This ensures that when you press a key, the desired character will be displayed, and the same character will be printed by your printer.

The process of matching ASCII codes against characters in a character set is called *mapping*. The following section describes how you map a set of numbers onto a set of characters so that they correspond exactly to each other.

Numbering Systems

Computers use a variety of numbering systems to operate. The most basic numbering system is the binary system, in which there are only two digits, 0 and 1. The digital circuitry used in computers operates by using small voltages that turn magnetic bits on or off. Therefore, 0 and 1 are used to represent the two states of off and on, respectively.

Counting in binary is not difficult, but it does require some adjustment from the standard decimal-numbering scheme. The progression of numbers and their matching decimal conversions are shown in Table E.3.

The general rule for converting numbers from binary to decimal is to multiply the number in every binary number column by 2 raised to the column-number power. You count column numbers from the right, starting with 0. For the binary number 1101, for example, you would obtain

$$(1 \times 2^0) + (0 \times 2^1) + (1 \times 2^2) + (1 \times 2^3)$$

where any number to the 0 power (2^0 in this case) is defined as equal to 1. This is called *counting in base 2*.

The *decimal* system counts in base 10. Using the same method of converting binary numbers, you can see that breaking down the decimal number 2014 into its component parts works like this:

$$(4 \times 10^0) + (1 \times 10^1) + (0 \times 10^2) + (2 \times 10^3)$$
$$= 4 + 10 + 000 + 2000$$
$$= 2014$$

Binary	Decimal
0	0
1	1
10	2
11	3
100	4
101	5
110	6
111	7
1000	8
1001	9
1010	10

Table E.3: Binary-to-decimal conversion

Another numbering system is called *octal,* or base 8. This system has only eight digits, 0 to 7. The octal number 701 is converted to base 10 (decimal) by the following computation:

$$(1 \times 8^0) + (0 \times 8^1) + (7 \times 8^2)$$
$$= 1 + 0 + 448$$
$$= 449$$

The last major numbering system in computers is called *hexadecimal,* which counts in base 16. This system has 16 digits in it: 0 to 9 and A to F, which form the counting sequence 0123456789ABC-DEF. To count in this system, you use the same method you use for other numbering systems. The hexadecimal number BA7 translates to decimal as

$$(7 \times 16^0) + (A \times 16^1) + (B \times 16^2)$$

which is equal to

$$7 + (10 \times 16^1) + (11 \times 16^2)$$

which is also equal to

$$7 + 160 + 2816$$
$$= 2983$$

Table E.4 demonstrates how to count in hexadecimal.

Hexadecimal notation is convenient for byte values because a hexadecimal digit is equivalent to 4 ($2^4 = 16$) binary digits (called a *nibble*) and there are 8 bits ($2^8 = 256$-character set) in a byte. A byte can therefore be represented by two hexadecimal digits.

Hexadecimal	Decimal
0	0
.	.
.	.
9	9
A	10
B	11
.	.
.	.
F	15
10	16
.	.
.	.
1A	26

Table E.4: Hexadecimal-to-decimal conversion

Selections from The SYBEX Library

DOS

The ABC's of MS-DOS
Alan R. Miller
224pp. Ref. 395-3
This plain-language guide for new or intermediate users treats everything from first start-up to customizing the system for day-to-day use. Includes useful utilities, plus tips on avoiding traps and recovering from errors.

Mastering DOS*
Judd Robbins
450pp. Ref. 400-3
This four-part, in-depth tutorial addresses the needs of users at all levels. Topics range from running applications, to managing files and directories, configuring the system, batch file programming, and techniques for system developers. A major book.

The MS-DOS Handbook (Second Edition)
Richard Allen King
339pp. Ref. 352-X
Two reference books in one, with separate sections for the programmer and the user. Topics include disk, screen and port control, batch files, networks, MS-DOS/PC-DOS compatibility, and more. Covers version 3.

MS-DOS Power Users Guide, Volume I (Second Edition)*
Jonathan Kamin
397pp. Ref. 345-7
Tips, techniques and programming utilities for high-performance systems. Configuring the system, redirecting I/O, disk, file and directory structures, hard disks, RAM disks, batch programming in depth, and the ANSI.SYS device driver.

Performance Programming Under MS-DOS
Michael J. Young
400pp. Ref. 420-8
Practical techniques for maximizing performance in MS-DOS software by making best use of system resources. Topics include functions, interrupts, devices, multitasking, memory residency and more, with examples in C and assembler.

The ABC's of PC-DOS*
Alan R. Miller
250pp. Ref. 438-0
A beginner's guide to PC-DOS for users of the IBM PC and compatibles – everything from working with disks and files, to using built-in commands, customizing the system, recovering from errors, and adding some handy utilities.

Essential PC-DOS (Second Edition)
Myril Clement Shaw/ Susan Soltis Shaw
332pp. Ref. 413-5
An authoritative guide to PC-DOS, including version 3.2. Designed to make experts out of beginners, it explores everything from disk management to batch file programming. Includes an 85-page command summary.

The IBM PC-DOS Handbook
Richard Allen King
340pp. Ref. 368-6
A guide to the inner workings of PC-DOS 3.2, for intermediate to advanced users and programmers of the IBM PC series. Topics include disk, screen and port control, batch files, networks, compatibility, and more.

SPREADSHEETS AND INTEGRATED SOFTWARE

The ABC's of 1-2-3 (Second Edition)
Chris Gilbert/Laurie Williams
245pp. Ref. 355-4

Online Today recommends it as "an easy and comfortable way to get started with the program." An essential tutorial for novices, it will remain on your desk as a valuable source of ongoing reference and support. For Release 2.

Mastering 1-2-3
Carolyn Jorgensen
466pp. Ref. 337-6

Get the most from 1-2-3 Release 2 with this step-by-step guide emphasizing advanced features and practical uses. Topics include data sharing, macros, spreadsheet security, expanded memory, and graphics enhancements.

Lotus 1-2-3 Desktop Companion (SYBEX Ready Reference Series)
Greg Harvey
976pp. Ref. 385-6

A full-time consultant, right on your desk. Hundreds of self-contained entries cover every 1-2-3 feature, organized by topic, indexed and cross-referenced, and supplemented by tips, macros and working examples. For Release 2.

Power User's Guide to Lotus 1-2-3*
Pete Antoniak/E. Michael Lunsford
400pp. Ref. 421-6

This guide for experienced users focuses on advanced functions, and techniques for designing menu-driven applications using macros and the Release 2 command language. Interfacing techniques and add-on products are also considered.

Lotus 1-2-3 Book of Style*
Tim K. Nguyen
350pp. Ref. 454-2

For users of 1-2-3 who want a definite and comprehensive guide to writing 1-2-3 spreadsheets in a stylistically correct and acceptable way. Lots of examples show how to create models that are powerful and efficient, yet easily understandable.

Mastering Lotus HAL
Mary V. Campbell
342pp. Ref. 422-4

A complete guide to using HAL "natural language" requests to communicate with 1-2-3—for new and experienced users. Covers all the basics, plus advanced HAL features such as worksheet linking and auditing, macro recording, and more.

Simpson's 1-2-3 Macro Library
Alan Simpson
298pp. Ref. 314-7

Increase productivity instantly with macros for custom menus, graphics, consolidating worksheets, interfacing with mainframes and more. With a tutorial on macro creation and details on Release 2 commands.

Data Sharing with 1-2-3 and Symphony: Including Mainframe Links
Dick Andersen
262pp. Ref. 283-3

The complete guide to data transfer between Lotus products (1-2-3 and Symphony) and other popular software. With an introduction to microcomputer data formats, plus specifics on data sharing with dBASE, Framework, and mainframe computers.

Mastering Symphony (Third Edition)
Douglas Cobb
840pp. Ref. 470-4

A complex program explained in detail. Includes version 1.2 with the new Macro Library Manager. "This reference book is the bible for every Symphony user I know...If you can buy only one book, this is definitely the one to buy." —IPCO Info

Focus on Symphony Macros
Alan Simpson
239pp. Ref. 351-1

An in-depth tutorial guide to creating, using, and debugging Symphony macros, including developing custom menus and automated systems, with an extensive library of useful ready-made macros for every Symphony module.

Focus on Symphony Databases
Alan Simpson/Donna M. Mosich
398pp. Ref. 336-8

Master every feature of this complex system by building real-life applications from the ground up—for mailing lists, inventory and accounts receivable. Everything from creating a first database to reporting, macros, and custom menus.

Better Symphony Spreadsheets
Carl Townsend
287pp. Ref. 339-2

Complete, in-depth treatment of the Symphony spreadsheet, stressing maximum power and efficiency. Topics include installation, worksheet design, data entry, formatting and printing, graphics, windows, and macros.

Andersen's Symphony Tips and Tricks (Second Edition)
Dick Andersen/Janet McBeen
321pp. Ref. 342-2

Hundreds of concise, self-contained entries point the way to optimal use of Symphony features, including troubleshooting tips. Covers all five Symphony modules, plus macros and the command language, and Release 1.1.

Mastering Framework II
Douglas Hergert/Jonathan Kamin
509pp. Ref. 390-2

This business-minded tutorial includes a complete introduction to idea processing, "frames," and software integration, along with its comprehensive treatment of word processing, spreadsheet, and database management with Framework.

Advanced Techniques in Framework: Programming in FRED
Alan Simpson
320pp. Ref. 246-9

This introduction to the FRED programming language is for experienced Framework users who need to expand their word processing, spreadsheet, graphics, and database management skills.

Mastering Enable*
Keith D. Bishop
350pp. Ref. 440-2

A comprehensive, practical, hands-on guide to Enable 2.0 integrated word processing, spreadsheet, database management, graphics, and communications—from basic concepts to custom menus, macros and the Enable Procedural Language.

Mastering Q & A
Greg Harvey
399pp. Ref. 356-2

This hands-on tutorial explores the Q & A Write, File, and Report modules, and the Intelligent Assistant. English-language command processor, macro creation, interfacing with other software, and more, using practical business examples.

Mastering SuperCalc 4
Greg Harvey
311pp. Ref. 419-4

A guided tour of this spreadsheet, database and graphics package shows how and why it adds up to a powerful business planning tool. Step-by-step lessons and real-life examples cover every aspect of the program.

Also:
Mastering SuperCalc 3
Greg Harvey
400pp. Ref. 312-0

Understanding Javelin PLUS
John R. Levine
Margaret Levine Young
Jordan M. Young
558pp. Ref. 358-9

This detailed guide to Javelin's latest release includes a concise introduction to business modeling, from profit-and-loss analysis to manufacturing studies. Readers build sample models and produce multiple reports and graphs, to master Javelin's unique features.

ACCOUNTING

Mastering DAC Easy Accounting*
E. Carl Merrifield
400pp. Ref. 442-9

This hands-on tutorial shows you how to run your own business accounting system from start to finish, using DAC Easy Accounting. Ideal for non-accounting professionals.

Advanced Techniques in AutoCAD*
Robert M. Thomas
350pp. Ref. 437-2
Develop custom applications using screen menus, command macros, and AutoLISP programming – no prior programming experience required. Topics include customizing the AutoCAD environment, advanced data extraction techniques, and much more.

FOR SCIENTISTS AND ENGINEERS

1-2-3 for Scientists and Engineers
William J. Orvis
450pp. Ref. 407-0
Fast, elegant solutions to common problems in science and engineering, using Lotus 1-2-3. Tables and plotting, curve fitting, statistics, derivatives, integrals and differentials, solving systems of equations, and more.

BASIC Programs for Scientists and Engineers
Alan R. Miller
318pp. Ref. 073-3
The algorithms presented in this book are programmed in standard BASIC code which should be usable with almost any implementation of BASIC. Includes statistical calculations, matrix algebra, curve fitting, integration, and more.

Turbo BASIC Programs for Scientists and Engineers
Alan R. Miller
375pp. Ref. 429-1
This practical text develops commonly-needed algorithms for scientific and engineering applications, and programs them in Turbo BASIC. Simultaneous solution, curve fitting, nonlinear equations, numerical integration and more.

Pascal Programs for Scientists and Engineers
Alan R. Miller
374pp. Ref. 058-X
Programming techniques are included for curve fitting, vector and matrix calculations, numerical integration, random number generation, statistical analysis, and more.

Turbo Pascal Programs for Scientists and Engineers
Alan R. Miller
332pp. Ref. 424-0
The author develops commonly-needed algorithms for science and engineering, then programs them in Turbo Pascal. Includes algorithms for statistics, simultaneous solutions, curve fitting, integration, and nonlinear equations.

FORTRAN Programs for Scientists and Engineers
Alan R. Miller
280pp. Ref. 082-2
In this collection of widely used scientific algorithms – for statistics, vector and matrix operations, curve fitting, and more – the author stresses effective use of little-known and powerful features of FORTRAN.

DATABASE MANAGEMENT

Mastering Paradox (Second Edition)
Alan Simpson
463pp. Ref. 375-9

Comprehensive treatment of Paradox versions 1.0 and 1.1 from database basics to command file programming with PAL. Topics include advanced queries and reports, automatic updating, and managing multiple data tables.

Mastering Reflex
Robert Ericson/Ann Moskol
336pp. Ref. 348-1

A complete introduction to Reflex: The Analyst, with hands-on tutorials and sample applications for management, finance, and technical uses. Special emphasis on its unique capabilities for crosstabbing, graphics, reporting, and more.

dBASE III PLUS Programmer's Reference Guide (SYBEX Ready Reference Series)
Alan Simpson
1056pp. Ref. 382-1

Programmers will save untold hours and effort using this comprehensive, well-organized dBASE encyclopedia. Complete technical details on commands and functions, plus scores of often-needed algorithms.

The ABC's of dBASE III PLUS
Robert Cowart
264pp. Ref. 379-1

The most efficient way to get beginners up and running with dBASE. Every 'how' and 'why' of database management is demonstrated through tutorials and practical dBASE III PLUS applications.

Mastering dBASE III PLUS: A Structured Approach
Carl Townsend
342pp. Ref. 372-4

In-depth treatment of structured programming for custom dBASE solutions. An ideal study and reference guide for applications developers, new and experienced users with an interest in efficient programming.

Also:

Mastering dBASE III: A Structured Approach
Carl Townsend
338pp. Ref. 301-5

Understanding dBASE III PLUS
Alan Simpson
415pp. Ref. 349-X

A solid sourcebook of training and ongoing support. Everything from creating a first database to command file programming is presented in working examples, with tips and techniques you won't find anywhere else.

Also:

Understanding dBASE III
Alan Simpson
300pp. Ref. 267-1

Understanding dBASE II
Alan Simpson
260pp. Ref. 147-0

Advanced Techniques in dBASE III PLUS
Alan Simpson
454pp. Ref. 369-4

A full course in database design and structured programming, with routines for inventory control, accounts receivable, system management, and integrated databases.

Also:

Advanced Techniques in dBASE III
Alan Simpson
505pp. Ref.282-5

Advanced Techniques in dBASE II
Alan Simpson
395pp. Ref. 228-0

Simpson's dBASE Tips and Tricks (For dBASE III PLUS)
Alan Simpson
420pp. Ref. 383-X

A unique library of techniques and programs shows how creative use of built-in features can solve all your needs – without expensive add-on products or external languages. Spreadsheet functions, graphics, and much more.

Simpsons's dBASE III Library
Alan Simpson
362pp. Ref. 300-7

A goldmine of techniques and ready-made programs to expand the off-the-shelf power of dBASE. Includes tutorials on command file programming, plus routines for finance, statistics, graphics, screens, oversize databases, and much more.

Expert dBASE III PLUS
Judd Robbins/Ken Braly
423pp. Ref. 404-6

Experienced dBASE programmers learn scores of advanced techniques for maximizing performance and efficiency in program design, development and testing, database design, indexing, input and output, using compilers, and much more.

Understanding R:BASE System V
Alan Simpson
499pp. Ref. 394-5

This complete tutorial guide covers every R:BASE function, while exploring and illustrating the principles of efficient database design. Examples include inventory management, mailing list handling, and much more.

Also:
Understanding R:BASE 5000
Alan Simpson
413pp. Ref. 302-3

Power User's Guide to R:BASE System V*
Alan Simpson
350pp. Ref. 354-6

A tutorial guide to structured programming in R:BASE, including system design, procedure files, performance issues and managing multiple data tables. With complete working systems for mailing list, inventory and accounts receivable.

GENERAL UTILITIES

The ABC's of the IBM PC
Joan Lasselle/Carol Ramsay
143pp. Ref. 102-0

Hands-on experience – without technical detail – for first-time users. Step-by-step tutorials show how to use essential commands, handle disks, use applications programs, and harness the PC's special capabilities.

Business Graphics for the IBM PC
Nelson Ford
259pp. Ref. 124-1

A complete guide to business graphics programming in IBM PC BASIC. Sample programs illustrate line, bar, and column charts, logarithm and scatter graphs, how to rotate, size and move graphs, printing, plotting and more.

Mastering ThinkTank on the IBM PC
Jonathan Kamin
350pp. Ref. 327-9

A business-minded tutorial on "idea processing" with ThinkTank – from first outlines to advanced features. Examples include logging sales calls, maintaining a resume, and creating a marketing plan. With complete reference sections.

Power User's Guide to SideKick*
Albert Holt
250pp. Ref. 371-6

A goldmine of tips and uses of SideKick and SuperKey with custom programming and popular applications, including 1-2-3, dBASE, WordStar and Crosstalk XVI. Includes discussion of interrupts, compatibility, programming issues, and commonly wanted patches.

COMPUTER-AIDED DESIGN AND DRAFTING

Mastering AutoCAD
George Omura
645pp. Ref. 378-3

This tutorial introduction to computer-aided design and drafting with AutoCAD is for newcomers to CADD as well as AutoCAD users seeking greater proficiency. An architectural project serves as an example throughout.

SYBEX Computer Books are different.

Here is why . . .

At SYBEX, each book is designed with you in mind. Every manuscript is carefully selected and supervised by our editors, who are themselves computer experts. We publish the best authors, whose technical expertise is matched by an ability to write clearly and to communicate effectively. Programs are thoroughly tested for accuracy by our technical staff. Our computerized production department goes to great lengths to make sure that each book is well-designed.

In the pursuit of timeliness, SYBEX has achieved many publishing firsts. SYBEX was among the first to integrate personal computers used by authors and staff into the publishing process. SYBEX was the first to publish books on the CP/M operating system, microprocessor interfacing techniques, word processing, and many more topics.

Expertise in computers and dedication to the highest quality product have made SYBEX a world leader in computer book publishing. Translated into fourteen languages, SYBEX books have helped millions of people around the world to get the most from their computers. We hope we have helped you, too.

For a complete catalog of our publications:

SYBEX, Inc. 2021 Challenger Drive, #100, Alameda, CA 94501
Tel: (415) 523-8233/(800) 227-2346   Telex: 336311